THE

HISTORY OF LAND TENURE
IN IRELAND.

T0349297

THE

HISTORY OF LAND TENURE

IN IRELAND.

BEING THE YORKE PRIZE ESSAY OF THE UNIVERSITY

OF CAMBRIDGE FOR THE YEAR 1888.

BY

WILLIAM ERNEST MONTGOMERY, M.A., LL.M.,

CLARE COLLEGE, CAMBRIDGE;

AND OF THE INNER TEMPLE, BARRISTER-AT-LAW.

CAMBRIDGE:

AT THE UNIVERSITY PRESS.

1889

CAMBRIDGE UNIVERSITY PRESS
Cambridge, New York, Melbourne, Madrid, Cape Town,
Singapore, São Paulo, Delhi, Mexico City

Cambridge University Press
The Edinburgh Building, Cambridge CB2 8RU, UK

Published in the United States of America by Cambridge University Press, New York

www.cambridge.org
Information on this title: www.cambridge.org/9781107696396

First published 1889
First paperback edition 2013

A catalogue record for this publication is available from the British Library

ISBN 978-1-107-69639-6 Paperback

PREFACE.

THE Yorke Prize was founded, under the sanction of the Court of Chancery, from the bequest of Edmund Yorke, M.A., late Fellow of St Catharine's College, Cambridge. It is awarded annually to such graduate of the University, of not more than seven years' standing from his first degree, as shall be the author of the best essay upon some subject relative to "The Law of Property, its Principles and History in various Ages and Countries." The subject announced for the year 1888 was "The History of Land Tenure in Ireland," and the following pages owe their existence to the conditions of the Prize which direct that the successful Essay shall be printed and published.

The immense range of an adequate history of Irish land tenure is manifest, and the present slight sketch can of necessity give but an outline of this involved subject. I may, however, briefly point out a few of the most prominent difficulties met with in tracing the troubled history of Irish land law, and explain the basis upon which the present Essay has been constructed. In the case of the Brehon Law there is undoubtedly a large opening for original work, but the initial difficulty inseparable from an entire dependence on translations, is enhanced by the complex nature of the Laws themselves. I have therefore when dealing with this branch of the subject given full references to the authorities relied on. Passing from the archaic law to English legislation I have throughout assumed that the forces of social disunion, which hindered the working of broad legislative measures, are of more importance than the multitude of petty and ineffectual experiments with Irish land law with which the Statute Book is crowded. Minor enactments have therefore been passed over in order to examine more fully those of extended scope.

The national, religious, and political bias which has coloured so much of the literature connected with Ireland creates an obstacle in the way of an attempt to write an impartial history of the land law. In addition much of the recent land legislation is so involved with current politics as to render it hard to avoid the vexed questions of the day. I have, however, endeavoured to the best of my ability to write without prejudice and to carefully eschew present political controversy.

WM. E. MONTGOMERY.

2, THE CLOISTERS,
PUMP COURT, TEMPLE.

CONTENTS.

PART I. IRELAND THE ENEMY.

PART II. IRELAND THE SLAVE.

PART III. THE IRELAND OF TO-DAY.

" No rule of law dealing with the contracts of owners and hirers of land is in itself objectively good or bad; the law which is most advantageous in one society would, if suddenly introduced into another, seem unjust, and probably prove mischievous; the good or evil effects of any law depend upon its being applicable or inapplicable to the social condition of the society into which it is introduced."—A. G. RICHEY.

" There has in general survived to the Irish farmer, through all vicissitudes, in despite of the seeming or real veto of the law, in apparent defiance of political economy, a living tradition of possessory right, such as belonged, in the more primitive ages of society, to the status of the man who tilled the soil."—*Report of the Bessborough Commission.*

PART I.

IRELAND THE ENEMY.

CHAPTER I.

The Agrarian Community of the Irish Celts.

The genesis of Irish social and political organization is found, said the late Sir Henry Maine, as in all the Aryan, Semitic, and Uralian races, to lie in the Family group[1]. Amongst the Irish Celts in the earliest times to which modern research has penetrated, a social organization built upon the actual or constructive kinship of members of the community, based on the real or theoretical descent from a common ancestor, can be traced. Such an organization finds its most perfect type in the joint family of modern India, (composed of those persons who would have taken part in the funeral ceremonies of the common ancestor), and corresponds to the Agnatic family of the Romans[2]. To the original conception of an organization of this nature the idea of individual property in the land is totally foreign; the rights of the individual being at most merely a more or less temporary usufruct of the soil by consent of the family group, the reversion remaining in the community. Peculiar interest, moreover, attaches to the development of the Irish agrarian system from the fact that the direct influence of that tremendous legislative engine the Roman Law has been absent[3], and even its indirect influence has been so slight that it may fairly be treated as unimportant[4]. Practically independent of ex-

---

[1] *Early History of Institutions*, pp. 65, 66. It is worthy of note that when the first English emigrants settled in New England, they distributed themselves in village communities.

[2] *Primitive Property*, Emile de Laveleye, p. 123. E. Hist. of Inst. pp. 106, 107.

[3] Mr Pearson says, "Ireland expiated dearly its independence of the Roman dominion, the secret of its long anarchy being in fact that it was Christianized without being civilized." *Hist. of Eng. during Early and Middle Ages*, Vol. I. p. 516.

[4] Sullivan's Intro. p. 5, *Manners and*

1—2

ternal pressure, primitive Aryan custom developed into a more advanced stage, and the theory of the family was extended and modified in the attempt to fit it to the needs of increasing population[1]. In the Brehon Laws (which will be more fully dealt with hereafter) exists a more or less fragmentary collection of some of the legal theory, if not practice, of this later stage of growth. It is endeavoured in this chapter to trace the expansion of the simple family system into the more complicated social organization presented by the Brehon Code ; and at the same time to mark the gradual development of separate ownership in the land, which at this later period was already being evolved from the original conception of corporate possession.

The Irish Celts, when ceasing to be nomad and settling upon definite areas of land, exercised apparently a social economy in which the possession of land may at first be deemed an accidental feature ; cattle constituting the only property to the possession of which much importance was attached, and remaining, even when property in land was held an integral item of the social system, the standard of value by which other things were calculated[2]. It would seem that in the earliest form of an ascertainable land system the head of the family group made a yearly or triennial allotment of lands[3] to the members of the family for the purpose of cultivation, and at the end of this period a redistribution was made. No right whatever was acquired by the allottee to the piece of land thus held

Customs of Ancient Irish, E. O'Curry. Of the Brehon Law it may also be said that it was uninfluenced by Roman law, despite that certain Roman law maxims are incorporated in the text, and that a Roman jurisconsult is mentioned, for these slight touches may be ascribed to contact with Churchmen. *E. Hist. of Inst.* p. 55.

[1] To this modification of the original theory of family unity we may ascribe the curious division of the Irish family into the Geilfine, Deirfine, Iarfine, and Indfine, together forming the Duthaig fine, or the sept in its narrower sense, as found in the Brehon laws.

[2] *Celtic Scotland*, Vol. III. c. iv. Skene.

[3] Prof. Sullivan and the writers of the school who have endeavoured with but little foundation to magnify the civilization of the early Irish Celts, hold that the tribe-land was universally held in severalty at the time of the Brehon laws, and that these periodical allotments extended only to the common lands.

for a year, he had merely by consent the usufruct thereof for such time. The tribal group is but an enlarged model of the family group, the members of the original cluster being represented by the allied sub-groups. Thus in its full expansion the tribe or fine[1] is found, with a chieftain or king at its head, formed of an aggregate of groups each a miniature of the larger tribe, and in their turn composed of other clusters until the lowest item of the social organization is reached in the family group or sept[2]. Such sept being the unit of a society[3] in which an individual as distinct from a member of a family group had scarcely in theory a proprietary existence. The mode of dealing with the land gradually underwent change, the yearly allotment passed into an allotment for life, the reversion being in the sept. It should be remembered, however, that in early times the portions of land allotted to members

---

[1] "The term 'fine' or 'family' is used to designate all subdivisions of Irish society, the tribe in its largest extent, the sept or the sub-tribe." *Systems of Landholding*, C. D. Field, p. 239.

Sir H. Maine held that the 'fine' translated 'tribe' in the *Corus Bescna* was the sept. In the *Tripartite Life of St Patrick*, where information might have been hoped for, no direct light is thrown upon the subject (see Vol. I. p. clxviii.).

[2] Mr F. Seebohm says, "A sept consisted of a number of actual or reputed *blood relations* bearing the same family names, and bound together by other and probably more artificial ties, such as common liability for the payment of eric, or blood fines." *The English Village Community*, c. vii. p. 219. The exact model of the sept is the joint family of modern India. It is a corporate, self-supporting unit, with "a perpetual existence like a society in mortmain;" it is "a juristic person and holds and acquires property;" its continuity depends on the land occupied by it, "but it is not merely a land-owning body, it has live chattels and dead chattels distinguished from those of individual tribesmen. Nor is it purely a cultivating body, it may follow a professional calling." Maine, Laveleye, Field.

From surveys of the country as late as the year 1600, in which the names of tenants are given, it is evident that they were blood relations, "with a carefully preserved genealogy guarding the fact of their relationship and consequent position in the tribe." Seebohm. " Survey of County Monaghan in 33 Eliz." *Inquisitiones Cancellariae Hiberniae* II. pp. xxi. and xxiii. and extract therefrom quoted at p. 216, Seebohm.

[3] Mr Skene, however, holds that the tuath or tribe preceded the sept, and ascribes the origin of the fine or sept, which is found at the time of the Brehon Laws, not in any way to a development of family relations, but to what may be termed the wealth-family of the Bo-Aire and his dependents. See *Celt. Scot.* Vol. III. p. 171.

of the tribe would form but a comparatively small portion
of the tribal territory, which would be divided into (1) pasturage ground held by the tribe in common, (2) unoccupied and
waste lands at first common property but in later times much
trenched upon by the chief, (3) the usufructuary allotments
of arable land[1].

The mode of succession to land at the time of the Brehon
Laws was the custom of Gavelkind[2], by which on the death
of a member of the sept the portion of land which had been
allotted to him passed back into the general stock and the chief
made a redistribution. It is pointed out by Mr Seebohm that
the clustering of households so frequently met with in the early
Irish surveys, and the runrig[3] form of the open field allotments,
were the natural modes of conducting a co-operative and shift-
ing agriculture[4]. In the ancient Irish law it is clear that
though the tribe is settled on the land, it yet holds, and is influenced by, ideas derived from the time when kinship and not
property was the bond between its members—this being the
explanation of Gavelkind succession. It is only necessary to
imagine the bonds of kinship further relaxed, and the connection of each family to the land strengthened till the temporary allotment to the household has become its actual property,

---

[1] See Skene, *Celt. Scot.* Vol. III. p.
139.

[2] And as regards the chieftain "Tanistry," this will be dealt with later.
Gavelkind is from gabhail-cine=ac-
cepted from the tribe. Although originally upon a death all the lands in
the sept were re-distributed, eventually
it would seem that only the lands held
by the deceased were so dealt with.
(Field.) The custom of Gavelkind was
thus described by Sir John Davies—
"Issint les terres de nature de gavelkind
ne fueront partibles enter le prochen
heires males de cesty qui morust sei-
sie, mes enter touts les males de son
sept en cest manner. Le canfinny, ou
chief del sept, fesait toutes les partitions per son discretion. Cest can-

finny après le mort de chescun terte-
nant que avait competent portion de
terre, assemblait tout le sept, et aiant
mis touts lour possessions en hotch-
pot fesait nouvel partition de tout : en
quel partition il ne assignait a les fils
de cesty que mourust le portion que
lour pere avait; mes il allotait al chas-
cun del sept solonque son antiquity."
Davies' Reports : *Le Irish Custome de
Gavelkind* (quoted Laveleye).

[3] Rundale, runrigg or runacre (said
to be derived from Celtic roinn-diol,
i.e. having a share in distribution :
Laveleye)...Similar systems prevailed
till quite lately in the Scottish High-
lands. *E. Hist. of Inst.* p. 101.

[4] *English Village Community*, Seebohm, p. 230.

to see the basis of the English custom of Gavelkind which is often erroneously contrasted with the archaic Irish mode of succession bearing the same name. But though this custom of Gavelkind (in its large sense) was still at the time of the Brehon Laws generally accepted as the theory of succession to land, and the proprietary rights were theoretically vested in the community, there is evidence to prove that much individual property actually existed; so much so indeed that at the end of the 10th or beginning of the 11th century the Irish people were in a state of transition from common property to several ownership, the Brehon writers themselves rather favouring the theory of private property[1].

Many causes went to produce this alteration in the nature and conception of ownership. As a primary factor in causing the change stands the increase of population, aided by the fact that in certain instances the temporary occupation of tribe-land by the individual tended, through the sufferance or consent of the community, to become permanent[2]: lasting possession being probably generated by the scarcity of land rendering a higher degree of cultivation necessary than the periodical division every year or every three years would allow, and the extra labour expended fostering the idea of property[3]. In addition, a change which took place in the social organization of society, namely the increase in the power of the chief, had a large influence in breaking up the archaic theory of communism in the soil[4]. The original notion of Father of the community

---

[1] The book of the Dun Cow (Lebor na Huidre) compiled in the 7th century by the Abbot of Clanmacnois, known to us in an Irish MS. of the year 1100, says "Round the field there was neither ditch, hedge, nor stone wall, and the land was not divided till came the period of the sons of Aed Slane (7th cent.), but only smooth fields....It was in consequence of the great number of families at this time that divisions and boundaries of the soil were introduced in Ireland." Seebohm, p. 225 and *Prim. Prop.* Laveleye, p. 125.

[2] *E. Hist. of Inst.* p. 95.

[3] *Prim. Prop.* p. 125.

[4] "It may now, however, be laid down without rashness that Property in Land, as known to communities of the Aryan race, has had a twofold origin. It has arisen partly from the disentanglement of the individual rights of the kindred or tribesmen from the collective rights of the Family or Tribe, and partly from the growth and transmutation of the sovereignty of the Tribal Chief." *E. Hist. of Inst.* p. 120.

became merged in that of Leader of the clan, and even the idea of kinship amongst members of the tribe was assimilated to that of a bond of subjection to a common authority, in the further growth of which idea lies the root of the pseudo-clanship of the fuidhir tenants[1].

In order to understand the position of the chief with regard to the land it is necessary to appreciate the mode of succession to the chieftaincy—as regulated by the custom of Tanistry. A chief was elected for life by the whole tribe or sept, usually by show of hands, and his successor was in most cases chosen in the same way[2] during his lifetime. Though this successor (who when elected was termed the 'Tanaist') was nominally supposed to be the next of blood who was eldest and worthiest[3], it is easy to see how great weight the wishes of the existing ruler would have in regulating the choice of the clan. It is evident that a door was here opened for easy inroad on the corporate ownership of the tribe-land. When the Tanaist was a near relation of the then chief, landed property held by such chief in his private capacity would be likely on his death to be continued to his descendants with a lofty disregard of the customs of Gavelkind. Moreover even if it were appropriated by the Tanaist on his accession to the chieftaincy as being part of the appanage of office, and thus his due by the custom of Tanistry, it would by increasing the vassals and hence the power of the new ruler render further depredation by him from the tribe the more easy. The chief on election became, by virtue of such election, the proprietor of a seigniory over all

---

[1] Post, pp. 9, 17.

[2] Field, p. 242....When the claimant was powerful even the form of election was occasionally dispensed with. It is hard to overrate the power of 'the strong man armed' in troublous times. Strongbow himself is said to have been raised to the post of Roydamna during the lifetime of Dermot MacMurrough and hence to have claimed to succeed him. Hume says "The usual title of each petty sovereign was the murder of his predecessor."

[3] The Cain. Aigillne A. L. of I. Vol. II. p. 279 says "The head of every tribe...should be the man of the tribe who is the most experienced, the most noble, the most wealthy, the wisest, the most learned, the most truly popular, the most powerful to oppose, the most steadfast to sue for profits and to be sued for losses." The chieftaincy being elective, a power seems also to have rested with the clan, and to have been sometimes exercised, of removing a chief for mal-administra-

the lands of the tribe, and his power was greater still over the waste-lands[1]. From these latter, indeed, more than from inequitable re-allotment of occupied tribe-lands, it is probable that his accession of those allodial[2] lands was made, which by the facilities they offered for the support of his retainers and servile dependents became the mainstay of his power and the stepping-stone to increased conversion of tribal territory into private property. The very nature of the tribal system fostered this germ of despotism, for recurring once again to the archaic theory of the family community, and endeavouring to realize what was the position of a member who from any cause was expelled from its charmed circle, it is found that becoming a very Ishmael without a social, political, or legal existence no course was open to him but to endeavour to assimilate himself by some means to another kindred association. The only means by which this could be accomplished was by becoming the personal retainer of some chief, who in return for his services would give protection, and by subjection to whose authority he would gain a pseudo-kinship with the members of the tribe. In this way arose the class of Fuidhirs, strangers or fugitives from other tribes; and the tribal chief who extended his aegis over the outcast would in all probability allot for his use a portion of the waste-land of the tribe[3]. Such land, held theoretically at the will of the tribe, but practically from the chief, in return probably for military or agricultural service, soon became looked upon as a portion of the chief's demesnes (if it

tion. See case of Donell O'Garmleay, quoted p. 70, Vol. ii. of Ware's Antiquities of Ireland.

[1] Whilst dealing with the various causes that broke up the theory of common ownership and established severalty, it must be remembered that on the waste-lands near the border, cultivators of servile status were permitted to squat, and cultivating settlements of tribesmen occasionally took possession thereof; in many of these cases something resembling individual property arose. See on this

subject E. Hist. of Inst. p. 93.

[2] It is surely justifiable to use this term here.

[3] As is pointed out by Mr Justice Field, the 'Senchus Mor' alludes to three rents, a rack rent or extreme rent from one of a strange tribe (the Fuidhir), a fair rent from one of the tribe, the stipulated rent paid alike by him of the tribe and him of a strange tribe. Landholding and the relation of Landlord and Tenant in various countries. 2nd Ed. p. 240. See also E. Hist. of Inst.

is admissible to use the English manorial term); and the absolute dependence of the fuidhir tenant is well shown by the passages in the Brehon Law[1] sanctioning distress from a chief who did not aid his fuidhir against injustice.

In addition to his seigniory over the lands of the tribe, and his more extensive power over the waste-lands of the community, the chief had also certain lands allotted to him in a special way as appurtenant to his state, termed mensal lands, and these descended from chief to chief according to the custom of Tanistry as the appanage of office[2]. In these lands, separated from the common stock to support the dignity of the chieftaincy, is to be traced one of the very earliest signs of the decay of the system of corporate possession by the tribe, and in all probability the lever which opened the door to the earliest instances of separate property. The great power possessed by the chief over the tribe and the unsettled state both of society and law makes it apparent that the lands which were given as an attribute of the chieftaincy as to a corporation sole would be very liable to be retained by the nearest relatives of the chieftain in private ownership on his death.

By the time of the Brehon Laws the power of the chief had so increased over certain members of the tribe as to reduce them to a position of dependence[3] by the development of Saer and Daer tenancy, with the result that the lands originally occupied by them in ordinary common ownership with the rest of the clan had come to be held in many cases at what is equivalent to a rent. To properly understand the growth of these tenancies it is necessary to bear in mind that despite any amount of ultimate possession or control which was exercised over the land by the head of the clan, the germ of his power lay in the possession of cattle. These, the natural spoil of war to the conquering chief, were in the early agricultural community of more intrinsic value than land, of which there was at first a surplusage[4]; and it is in a great measure to the power

---

[1] Sen. Mor (*A. L. of I.* Vol. I. pp. 125 and 139).

[2] *E. Hist. of Inst.* p. 92.

[3] Much as the Patrician obtained power over the Plebeian debtor. *Land*

System of Ireland, Law Quarterly Review, 1887, pp. 135 and 136. O'Connor Morris.

[4] One is struck instantly in the Brehon Law, with the immense import-

over a tribesman acquired by the chief to whom he was indebted for a loan of cattle, that the origin of the idea of rent
for the soil may be traced[1].

Saer and Daer stock tenancies are the names given to the
relation subsisting between chief and tribesman, when a loan
of cattle has been advanced by the former to the latter; the
difference between Saer and Daer tenancy resting in the fact
that in the first where only a portion of the tenant's stock is
provided by the chief the tenant debtor remains a freeman, in
the latter where all the stock is found he becomes a villanus[2]
or at any rate is in a semi-servile state. Such loans, probably
one of the most formidable agencies in increasing the power of
the chief, were it would appear largely imposed upon those who
being tribesmen were obliged to receive the charge from their
head[3], and were always resorted to by those whose poverty prevented the acquisition of cattle (that is of the means of tillage)
by independent means. The complicated rules of these tenancies
will be referred to later on when the enactments of the Brehon
Law will be more fully dealt with. Here they are only important in so far as they represent another factor in the
influences breaking down the theory of common ownership
of the soil by the clan, and laying the foundation of ownership
of land held from a chief. The inroad made by these tenancies
upon the original theory of tribal constitution becomes far
more apparent when it is found that they were not confined to
chief and tribesmen of one clan, but might be created between

---

ance attached to the possession of
cattle.

[1] Sir H. Maine held that the rent
payable in the produce of the stock
and refections ultimately became a
rent payable in respect of the land.
The stock lent was termed 'Taurcreic'
and the food rent 'Besa,' see *E. Hist.
of Inst.* p. 160, and Skene Vol. III.
p. 146.

[2] Field, pp. 241—242.

[3] Prof. Sullivan quotes the following
enactment of the Brehon Law. "It is
competent for a man never to accept

base wages from any man unless it be
his own will to do so, and it is competent for him not to accept Saerrath
(free wages) from anyone but from a
king, but he is not entitled to refuse
the free wages of his king. Every
man in the Tuath is bound to receive
the wages of the Rig Tuatha (king of
the territory)," and says "Theoretically speaking no freeman need become
the dependent of another save the
king of his territory, but the condition
of dependence was imposed upon him
by the circumstances of his position."

members of different clans; the tribesman of one becoming the Daer-stock tenant of another. The social connection between the chief and his tenants is stated in the Senchus Mor[1] to be "That he (the chief) is to give them stock and returnable 'seds,' and to protect them against every injustice that he is able, and they are to render him victuals and labour, and respect, and to return the 'seds' to his heir, or for his heir where it is right *(to do so)*. The chief has *(power to pronounce)* judgment, and proof, and witness, upon his Daer-stock tenants; but his Saer-stock tenants can oppose them, and bear witness against his tenants if they be impartial witnesses." These Saer and Daer tenancies are also important in their bearing on the modifications of the land system, for their tendency was undoubtedly to reduce the debtor to vassalage; and in this fact probably lies the explanation of the origin of many of the complicated servile groups with which we are confronted in the Brehon Laws and in all early Irish history[2].

The theory of common ownership recognized no right of alienation by the individual of his share of the tribe-land[3], and even in the Brehon Laws this doctrine holds, "every tribesman is able to keep his tribe-land, he is not to sell it, or alienate it, or conceal it, or give it to pay for crimes or contracts"[4]. The original universality of the rule was, however, infringed by exceptions and in certain cases a portion at least of his tribe-land might be alienated by the tribesman by grant, contract, or bequest. As regards the property which his own effort had acquired, a larger power of alienation was possessed by the tribesman than he had over that obtained by allotment. Again in the Corus Bescna a still further distinction is drawn between the property which a man has acquired by special industry and that which is merely the produce of the land in the ordinary course of husbandry, the former being regarded as more

[1] *Ancient Laws of Ireland*, Vol. II. p. 345.

[2] "It is by taking stock that the free Irish tribesman becomes the Ceile or Kyle, the vassal or man of his chief, owing him not only rent but service and homage. The exact effects of

'commendation' are thus produced." *E. Hist. of Inst.* p. 158.

[3] Save by consent of the community.

[4] *A. L. of I.* Vol. II. p. 283, and see *E. Hist. of Inst.* p. 108.

particularly his own property and hence his right of alienation
being greater over it. An examination of the Brehon Laws
shows that there can be little doubt that the growth of this
power of alienation found if not its origin at least its most
fostering element in the influence of the Church[1]. How early
such influence began to work it is impossible to say, for there is
negative evidence that for some time after the arrival of St
Patrick Christianity had not spread throughout Ireland[2]. Still
it is certain that beginning from about the time of St Patrick
the ecclesiastical element entered the Irish legal system, and
many of the increased facilities for the alienation of land, and
much of the advancement of the idea of the binding nature of
contract are due to the efforts of the monks. The Christian
influence on the law tended in the direction of increasing the
property of the Church, with a view to which it favoured freedom of alienation. Thus despite that the Brehon Law lays
down that 'no tribesman is to sell, alienate, or conceal his
tribe-land or to give it to pay for his crimes or contracts[3],' yet
under certain circumstances exceptions were made, and in its
original conception the grantee contemplated is without doubt
the Church[4] which is indebted to this source for its termon
lands.

The position of the Church with regard to the land at the
time of the Brehon Laws is thus explained in the Senchus
Mor[5], "The social connection which subsists between the church

---

[1] A curious side light is thrown
on this by the fact that in the *Tripartite Life of St Patrick*, the word for
bequest occurs four times and always
in connection with ecclesiastics.

[2] For example see a passage in the
Annals of the Four Masters, Vol. I.
pp. 143, 145 (quoted in Pritchard's
Physical History of Mankind, p. 140),
where it is stated that Laeghaire, the
son of Niall, having been in the year
457 taken captive in a battle against
the inhabitants of Leinster, swore by
the sun and the wind that he would
never again demand a tribute for his
cows. The oath having been violated

he was killed by the sun and wind.

"Laeghaire, son of Niall, died
On the side of Caissi, green its
land;
The elements of God, whose guarantee he had violated,
Inflicted the doom of death upon
the king."

This quatrain is quoted in The *Four
Masters*, p. 145, and also in *Lebor na
Huidre*, but the author is unknown.

[3] *A. L. of I.* Vol. II. p. 283.

[4] *E. Hist. of Inst.* p. 108.

[5] *Sen. Mor* (*A. L. of I.* Vol. II.
pp. 345 and 347).

and its tenants of ecclesiastical lands is, preaching and offering:—and requiem is due from the church to its tenants of ecclesiastical lands, and the receiving of every son for instruction, and of every (*such*) tenant to right repentance; tithes, and first fruits, and alms, are due of them to her, and full honor price when they are in strong health, and one-third honor price at the time of death; and the church has (*the power of pronouncing judgment*), and proof, and witness upon its tenants of ecclesiastical land, both Saer-stock tenants and Daer-stock tenants; and upon every other layman, even though he be a Saer-stock tenant of ecclesiastical lands, unless there is another church of equal dignity claiming him." This extract shows conclusively how large a temporal power had been acquired by the Church, and it is plain how potent an influence it must have exerted in moulding the Brehon Law. It is far from improbable also that the power of the Church was felt in the local laws which influenced petty communities to a larger extent than is shown by the laws of Tara. Mr Skene, who lays stress on the laxity of sexual relations in the earliest times of Irish history, would also ascribe in the main to the influence of the Christian church[1] the practical creation of the paternal power[2], and would defer till this time the real existence of the family group with the father as its head. It seems probable, however, even if the marriage bond was not held binding, that he has underrated the eagerness with which sons (the warriors of the future) and daughters (by whose means valuable alliances could be contracted) would be claimed by the father as members of his family[3].

Though the various causes[4] which tended to break down the original theory of family unity, to disintegrate collective

[1] The Early Irish Ecclesiastical Law limited marriage relations strictly. Canones S. Patricii (*Councils and Ecclesiastical documents of Great Britain and Ireland*, A. W. Hodden and W. Stubbs). ii. Synod xxv—xxviii. See *The Celtic Church* by F. E. Warren.

[2] Skene's *Celt. Scot.* Vol. iii. p. 138.

[3] "The 'Book of Aicill' provides for

the legitimation not only of the bastard, but of the adulterine bastard, and measures the compensation to be paid to the putative father." *E. Hist. of Inst.* p. 59.

[4] The influence of the more advanced civilization of foreign nations was scarcely felt by the early Irish community, and is only treated of in two

ownership and to establish the theory of several possession, have been touched on, it must not be imagined that in the Brehon Laws ownership in severalty was recognized as the rule. On the contrary the property, social, and juristic rights of individuals are still theoretically merged in the system of the family group, but the numerous exceptions which are apparent show clearly the effects of the attacks made on the original conception of ownership. There is clearly traceable the progress of what may be termed the natural feudalization of the land, retarded indeed by the want of a strong centralized government and doomed never to be consummated in the natural order of things, (since the Brehon Law was roughly rooted up, and a more advanced system thrust on a nation unfit to receive it) but undeniably present.

Before commencing an examination of the extant tracts of the Brehon Law it is necessary to treat more fully than has yet been done of the relation of the landholding classes between themselves in early Irish society.

In the earliest times the inhabitants of Ireland are found divided into the two great classes, free and unfree[1], and these two classes seem to have been divided into many grades. Amongst the free the division is one which may almost be termed that of the "classes and masses." The former order, the Aires, being again subdivided into the two classes of (1) Flaths and (2) Bo-Aires[2]. The Flaths represented an aristocracy of

instances in this essay (1) where the influence of the Church is incidentally dealt with in this and the following chapter, (2) where the effect of the establishment of the Colony of the Pale is treated of in chapters III. and IV.

[1] "The acts of the Council of Armagh in 1171 show that there had been a custom of buying Anglo-Saxons from merchants robbers and pirates; for it was decreed ' ut Angli ubique per insulam servitatis vinculo mancipati in pristinam revocentur libertatem.' " (See Sigerson quoting Girald. Camb. *Expugnatio Hibernica*, L. I. c. xviii.) Some very ancient Canons

of the Church (quoted c. 20 Ware) also point to this, and we learn from Seyer's *History of Bristol* that slaves were exported from England even as late as the reign of King John. See also William of Malmesbury *de Vit Wlstani*. In the *Book of Rights*, printed by the Celtic Society, p. 174, and quoted by Skene in Vol. III. p. 140, the legendary origin of the class of the unfree is given. In the main slavery was due to the successive waves of conquest and to the effect of internal wars.

[2] See Sullivan's Intro. to O'Curry, pp. c. and ci.

birth, their wealth lying in land and their rank being hereditary; whilst the Bo-Aires or Cow-Aires represented an aristocracy of wealth, or those who from the amount of their possessions in cattle rose above the ordinary tribesman, and whose descendants under certain circumstances were capable of rising to the rank of Flaths. These two classes of Aires alone possessed to the full the rights of freemen[1], but the possession of sufficient wealth entitled any free native to become a Bo-Aire. The ordinary free tribesman was the Fer Midba, or inferior man, and of this class there are two divisions (1) those over the age of 14 and under 20, who though emancipated were not in possession of their full privileges, and (2) those over the age of 20, entitled to a separate residence and a share of the tribe-land[2].

When the tribesman had received a loan of cattle he became a member of the class of Ceiles. The Ceiles were divided into the Saer, that is free, Ceiles and the Daer or base Ceiles. The relation of these two classes to the chief to whom they were indebted for the loan of cattle has been already remarked under the short description given of Saer and Daer stock holdings, and will be more fully dealt with later. Although the Daer Ceiles were base tenants they were yet possessed of certain definite rights in the tribe and in the tribal territory, and in this were widely separated from the servile classes of the Bothacks, Sencleiths and Fuidhirs whose rights were few, and who were almost in a state of complete servitude[3]. These latter classes cultivated what in default of a better word may be termed the chief's demesnes, and possessed no political rights.

"The Bothacks[4] or Cottiers, Saer and Daer, had a right of settlement, served the land noble as hired and farm labourers and performed menial services[5]." The Sencleiths appear to have been old adherents of the Flath, the descendants of old and

---

[1] See Sullivan's Intro. to O'Curry, p. cix.

[2] See Skene's *Celt. Scot.* Vol. III. p. 143.

[3] Sullivan's Intro. to O'Curry, p. cxv.

[4] Bothack from Both, a shed or cabin. Prof. Sullivan says that the Saer

Bothacks seem to have been possessed of no property save a cabin on the lands of the Flath whom they served; the Daer Bothacks were farm labourers.

[5] Sigerson's *History of Land Tenures and Land Classes in Ireland*, p. 9.

privileged servants or persons who at some time by favour had acquired a right to settle on the demesne[1]. The Fuidhir or refugee tenants have been treated of before, but it should be noticed that a great point of difference existed between them and the classes of Bothacks and Sencleiths; for whilst the latter formed part of the affiliated family or clan known in the Brehon Law as the 'Fine Flatha,' and were entitled as of right to sustenance, habitation, and to the usufruct of the soil, the former class were strangers and outcasts, their rights in the clan, if any, being based on a contract with its chief. The free Fuidhirs indeed possessed in some degree the rights of freemen, being in reality strangers from other tribes, who, in consideration of only holding their Fuidhir tenancy of the land from year to year[2], were allowed to retain certain rights. The Daer Fuidhirs on the other hand[3] were in all respects in a position of the most servile dependence and were the victims of great hardships, their rights and liabilities being in almost all cases merged in those of the Flath on whom they were dependent, and whose chattels to all intents and purposes they were. These Daer Fuidhirs were mostly prisoners taken in war[4], escaped criminals who had been given shelter, defaulting debtors, and outcasts of every kind. It seems, however, that a man might voluntarily become a Daer Fuidhir, and that he might become so for a limited number of years; while a family of this class who remained nine times nine years on the land became entitled to rank with the Sencleiths. The following table purports to show the relation of the social orders of the tribe[5] or Tuath.

---

[1] For example mercenaries.

[2] Prof. Sullivan says "If he entered into longer engagements than one year with another than his own chief he lost his rights and became permanently a Fuidhir." Intro. to O'Curry, p. cxxv.

[3] The Brehon Law draws a very sharp line of demarcation between the Saer and Daer Fuidhir.

[4] St Patrick was of this class when he was first brought to Ireland.

[5] This table is put forward with diffidence the subject being much involved. For authorities see Skene, Vol. iii. p. 142—147, also *Ancient Laws*, Vol. iv. p. 299, also Sigerson and Sullivan. The classes of the Bo-Aires of which the Aire coisring "who represented the people before king and synod" was the highest, and the Ogaire or 'young lord' the lowest, differed merely in their degrees of wealth. The classes of the Flaths are based on the number of Ceile tenants each possessed, the Aire-forgaill being the most important

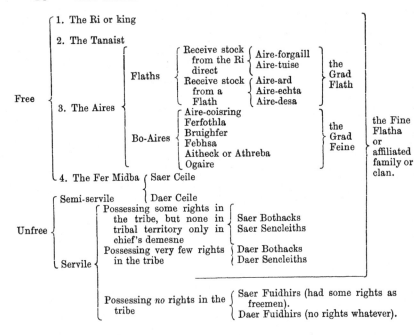

```
Free   ⎧ 1. The Ri or king
       ⎪ 2. The Tanaist
       ⎪                        ⎧ Flaths    ⎧ Receive stock   ⎧ Aire-forgaill ⎫
       ⎪                        ⎪           ⎪ from the Ri     ⎨ Aire-tuise    ⎬  the
       ⎪                        ⎪           ⎨ direct                            Grad
       ⎪                        ⎪           ⎪ Receive stock   ⎧ Aire-ard      ⎫  Flath
       ⎪ 3. The Aires ⎨         ⎪           ⎩ from a          ⎨ Aire-echta    ⎬
       ⎨                        ⎪             Flath            ⎩ Aire-desa     ⎭
       ⎪                        ⎪                                                        the Fine
       ⎪                        ⎪ Bo-Aires  ⎧ Aire-coisring                    ⎫         Flatha
       ⎪                        ⎪           ⎪ Ferfothla                         the     or
       ⎪                        ⎩           ⎨ Bruighfer                        ⎬ Grad   affiliated
       ⎪                                    ⎪ Febhsa                            Feine   family or
       ⎪                                    ⎪ Aitheck or Athreba               ⎭        clan.
       ⎪                                    ⎩ Ogaire
       ⎩ 4. The Fer Midba ⎧ Saer Ceile
                          ⎩ Daer Ceile
Unfree ⎧ Semi-servile
       ⎪           ⎧ Possessing some rights in   ⎧ Saer Bothacks
       ⎨           ⎪ the tribe, but none in      ⎨ Saer Sencleiths
       ⎪ Servile  ⎨ tribal territory only in    ⎧ Daer Bothacks
       ⎩           ⎪ chief's demesne             ⎨ Daer Sencleiths
                   ⎩ Possessing very few rights
                     in the tribe

                   ⎧ Possessing no rights in the ⎧ Saer Fuidhirs (had some rights as
                   ⎩ tribe                       ⎨   freemen).
                                                 ⎩ Daer Fuidhirs (no rights whatever).
```

and being also probably the Flath Geilfine or Geilfine chief. Though the above table gives the organization of a complete tribe, such tribe would not probably stand alone but would be linked by certain ties to other Tuaths, and the body thus constituted would represent that larger tribe known as the Mortuath.

CHAPTER II.

THE BREHON LAW.

HAVING sketched the various causes which chiefly tended in Ireland to mould into a more complex form the original conception of ownership by the clan, and the disintegrating influences which tended to develop ownership in severalty, it is proposed in this chapter to examine more carefully the exact nature of land holding as recognized by the Brehon Laws.

These Laws were the work of a particular class—the Brehons (*Brithemain*), a hereditary caste of lawyers. It has been suggested that these Brehons were substantially identical with the class of Druids found amongst the Celts of the Continent[1], and it may be that on the introduction of Christianity the Irish Druids concentrated their attention on the study and expansion of the laws, a subject which had formerly been only a portion of their duties[2]. This supposition goes far towards accounting for a great mass of semi-barbarous and semi-christian but altogether religious doctrine in the secular Brehon Law. It is specially noticeable as affording an explanation of the comparatively insignificant relation of the sanctions to various offences by suggesting the existence, at the time of the inception of the rules[3], of a moral sanction forming the understood complement of each material enactment and remedying its deficiencies.

[1] See *E. Hist. of Inst.* p. 35.

[2] The Sen. Mor ascribes the good judgments of the Brehon Law to the influence of the Holy Spirit on just men who were in the island of Erin before its conversion. *A. L. of I.* Intro. Vol. I. p. viii.

[3] Notice on this subject the late Sir H. Maine's remarks on "Sitting Dharna," and the statement in the Sen. Mor (*A. L. of I.* Vol. I. p. 113) that notice and fasting precede distress in the case of a chief.

Generally of Royal blood and standing in the relation of adviser to the chief[1], while in many cases little if at all his inferior in prestige[2]; the representatives of culture as opposed to crass ignorance, and claiming through St Patrick a semi-inspired origin for their legal rules[3], the Brehons in the earlier phases of Irish history possessed in themselves, and transmitted to their rules, an authority which it is hard for those trained in modern ideas to realize. The weight attaching to the dicta of the Brehon was the more remarkable as the system was based on mere voluntary references to arbitration[4], and as the sanction was a factor conspicuous mainly by its absence or insufficiency; while even when existent it appears to have been irregularly and intermittently enforced owing to the want of a strong centralized government.

The great antiquity of the system whose legal rules of social relations and public polity the Brehon Laws profess to expound and regulate, render it a matter of deep regret that there is a scarcity of ancient Irish MSS. The limited amount of authentic documents, however, is no matter of wonder when it is remembered that anarchy reigned supreme in early Irish history, and that the absence of walled towns and stone buildings rendered the preservation of manuscripts difficult; while, in addition, during the earlier part of the 18th century it was a serious matter to be as much as found in possession of an Irish book[5]. The Brehon Laws, as far as extant, consist of certain tracts, the text of which is glossed and expanded by later commentaries. Commissioners were appointed for the purpose of selecting and translating the Ancient Laws of Ireland, and the four volumes published by them contain translations of the Seṅchus Mor with its subtracts[6], the book of Aicill, the Crith Gabhlach, and

---

[1] *A. L. of I.* Vol. iv. p. 341.

[2] "For the king excels, for he can decide against every kind of person except those of the two orders of religion and learning who are of equal rank with himself." Sen. Mor, Gloss. *A. L. of I.* Vol. i. p. 85.

[3] See the account given by the Sen. Mor of the origin of the Brehon Law.

[4] See — in one of the prefaces to 3rd Vol. of *Ancient Laws.* In the Sen. Mor it is stated that any foreigner or stranger was entitled to be judged by any Brehon he might choose. *A. L. of I.* Vol. i. p. 7.

[5] Sullivan's Intro. to O'Curry, p. xix.

[6] The Senchus Mor is divided into

certain smaller tracts on judgments of co-tenancy, of divisions of
land, of divisions of the tribe and territory, of crimes, of rights
of water and so forth, with a tract on bee judgments. The
date of the ancient law tracts is very uncertain ; the Senchus
Mor is stated in the *Annals of the four Masters* to date at
438 A.D., but the principal extant Brehon manuscripts are probably not older than the 14th century, some being even as
recent as the beginning of the 15th[1]. The obsolete form of
language of much of their text, however, and the portions of
old versified law embedded in it, point to a probability of these
manuscripts being in the main transcripts from older writings,
many of the glosses being as much translations as explanations[2].
But even taking this into consideration the language in which
the manuscripts are written will not carry us back much
farther than the middle of the 9th century[3], and the late Sir
Henry Maine thought that the dates of the Senchus Mor and
the book of Aicill were the 11th and 10th centuries respectively.
The Senchus Mor itself indeed claims to have been coeval with
St Patrick ; and Professor Sullivan argues from the internal

---

(1) the law of distress, (2) Services of
Hostage Sureties, (3) Fosterage, (4)
the two laws of tenure Saer-Stock
(Cain Law) and Daer-Stock (Cain
Aigillne), (5) social connexions, (6)
customary law (Corus Bescna). The
remainder is lost but is supposed to
have consisted of a tract on fines for
stealing from a church or termon
lands.

[1] Dr O'Donovan translated a mar-
ginal note which purports to have been
written in 1350 on one of the Dublin
manuscripts of the Sen. Mor to show
that it existed at that time. It runs
" One thousand three hundred ten and
forty years from the birth of Christ to
this night; and this is the second year
since the coming of the plague into
Ireland. I have written this in the
twentieth year of my age. I am Hugh,
son of Conor Mac Egan, and whoever
reads it let him offer a prayer of mercy

for my soul. This is Christmas night,
and on this night I place myself under
the protection of the King of Heaven
and earth, beseeching that He will
bring me and my friends safe through
this plague."

[2] Prof. Sullivan instances the case
of Druim Gall, a legal scribe in the
county of Clare between 1509—1511,
who confessed he could not understand
the organization or functions of the
ancient courts of Ireland (at this date
the Irish laws were still in force in
Clare, which was the last part of Ireland where the judgment of a Brehon
was delivered) and says, " Here we
have decisive evidence of a considerable lapse of time between the period
when the courts were held in their
full state and the beginning of the 16th
century." Intro. to O'Curry, p. xv.

[3] *E. Hist. of Inst.* p. 12 ; Sullivan's
Intro. to O'Curry, p. xvi and xvii.

state of Ireland after the commencement of the Danish wars that the laws must be prior to the beginning of the 9th century, surmising that the three centuries after St Patrick (practically the only period of even comparative tranquillity which the early history of Ireland records) were the parents of the Brehon Laws. But it is open to doubt whether legal activity will only co-exist with political quiescence. If this is indeed the date of the Brehon Laws being first committed to writing, their codification may rather be ascribed to the stimulus given to intellectual activity by the educational influences of the Church.

The early Irish law has many strong points of similarity with the laws of Wales[1], subject, however, to the important difference that the influence of the to some extent authoritative central government, which has fixed its seal on the Welsh laws, is absent in the Brehon code. The comparison nevertheless is of value as illustrating with much clearness that the alleged differences between Aryan sub-races are rather differences in their degrees of development than essential discrepancies[2]. The Brehon Law, despite its pretensions to being a code, is rather "an accretion of rules which have clustered round an older nucleus[3]," portions of the ancient versified law being, as has been stated, incorporated in the Senchus Mor and the book of Aicill. The late Sir Henry Maine held that probably each tract was the property of some individual legal school and exhibited its particular tenets[4]. In support of this it should be remembered that these laws were not in reality a "legislative structure," but were composed of the dicta of certain learned Brehons[5] upon sets of facts, either submitted to them or hypothetically stated by them. This juridical interpretation stood alone as the source of the Brehon Law, and bears a strong surface

[1] See *Ancient Laws of Wales*, pub. by Comm.; *History of Wales*, by John Jones.

[2] *E. Hist. of Inst.* p. 96.

[3] *E. Hist. of Inst.* p. 10.

[4] *E. Hist. of Inst.* p. 16, and this would perhaps account for the way in which stress is laid in many cases on the name of a Brehon who passed a judgment, e.g. "Sean, son of Aighe, passed the first judgment concerning distress." Sen. Mor, *A. L. of I.* Vol. I. p. 79.

[5] *E. Hist. of Inst.* p. 24, instancing the book of Aicill, by its own statement composed of the judgments of two Brehons, Cormac and Cennfaeladh.

analogy to the "responsa prudentum" of the Roman law, but the difference caused by the absence in the former case of the machinery of the courts and the sanctioning power of a centralized government prevents any true similarity.

It is a matter of great difficulty to know what stress to lay upon individual statements in the tracts, for in not a few cases the rules have evidently been constructed through certain given facts having suggested a number of hypothetical cases to the mind of the Brehon, upon which, though the law is laid down with great nicety and assurance, it is hard to imagine it possessed of a binding force. In the absence of that authority which can only be existent in conjunction with a strong centralized government, bald statements of supposititious law[1], not sanctioned by immemorial custom, could scarcely have carried any widespread authority. Not a few of the cases given are so trivial as to strongly suggest that they were merely illustrative examples used by the Brehon to instruct his pupil in the expansion of particular rules[2]. This theory of development also possesses inherent probability, for had the aim of the Brehon lawyer been directed to ascertaining general principles instead of particular applications, a more advanced law would have been obtained, but the greatest proof of the genuine antiquity of the system would have been lost.

The difficulty of justly estimating the relative value of the statements of these archaic laws is increased by the fact that a large proportion of their contents have palpably been evolved by successive generations; partly from the pre-existing law tenets, either oral or written, of the founder of the school, but also partly from the real or imaginary needs of increasing population, enlarged learning, and more diffused culture. These later additions have been sheltered under the cloak of the founder's supposed semi-divine[3] infallibility, and have been

---

[1] "Much of the commentary is confessedly speculative, and does not represent any existing customary law." *A. L. of I.* Intro. Vol. iii. p. x.

[2] This is particularly noticeable in the tract on bee judgments.

[3] "The early Brehon, possessing in his own breast the whole law, assumed a mysterious character, and was treated as an inspired or quasi-divine personage." *A. L. of I.* Intro. Vol. iii. p. xxxi.

incorporated into his system by what may almost be termed mental 'commendation[1].' Another difficulty also is met with at the outset of an enquiry into the Brehon Law in the ambiguity of the meaning of the terms used : thus, to take a well-known example, the word 'fine' is used (1) to denote those related within certain degrees of consanguinity, (2) the lord and his relatives together with his dependent Ceiles and Fuidhirs, (3) the whole tribe in its broadest sense. The amount of confusion caused by this looseness of expression can be better imagined than described.

In the preceding chapter the classes of society which appear to have been in existence at the time of the Brehon Laws were dealt with, and the more or less complete disuse of the original practice of common possession of the tribe-land was traced. Turning now to the period of the fullest development of the archaic code it is striking how seemingly complex a social system is revealed, when the simplicity of the tribal system as described by Sir John Davies so many centuries later is remembered. The native land law recognized by the Attorney-General of James the First will be dealt with in a subsequent chapter, but it is perhaps possible that the explanation of its apparent discrepancies with the scheme revealed in the Brehon Law is to be found in the fact that Sir John Davies was content to deal with the broad outlines of the case presented to him, while many of the provisions of the ancient laws were theoretical rather than practical. The ancient Irish land system, when viewed in the light of the Brehon Laws, shows the 'Tuath,' or territorial possession of the tribe, divided into the following parts[2]:—

(1)   The 'Deis' or lands of inheritance (orba).
(2)   Office or 'mensal' lands.
(3)   'Termon' lands—the possessions of the Church.
(4)   Pasture lands.
(5)   Arable lands.

[1] Notice some remarks by the late Sir H. Maine in *Early Law and Custom* on literary fosterage as exemplified in the laws of Menu, poems of Homer (taking Grote's theory) and the Brehon laws. The Senchus Mor, however, was supposed to be sacred even to an innovating Brehon.

[2] See Skene, *Celt. Scot.* Vol. III. p. 148. It is the *territory* to which by this time the word Tuath is properly applied. The tribe is now 'Ciniol.'

The first group, that is the lands of inheritance, stand upon a new basis altogether foreign to the theory of the primal tribal community, and are either (1) the private possessions of the Ri, as distinguished from the mensal lands which he held as the appanage of office, or (2) the private possessions of the Aires (or rather Flaths) which were either (*a*) ancient allodial lands[1], or (*β*) had become property in severalty by prescription, or (*γ*) had been amassed by the Flath in the same manner as the Ri had gathered his more extensive possessions, or (*δ*) had been granted as the reward of public service, or (*ε*) had been granted originally for life, and not returned into the public stock on the death of the usufructuary.

It is doubtful if these inheritance lands were governed by any real rules of descent save that of possession by members of one family as apart from the tribe ; and it is probable that they devolved by that most potent of all titles in troublous times, the right of might.   On the death of the Flath, therefore, the most powerful member of his family would succeed to the lands; while the ingrained notion of common ownership would be still so fixed in the other members that they would hold themselves in theory, if not in fact, joint possessors with him ; and submitting by force of circumstances to his nominal succession, would gain a very practical share of the inheritance by quartering themselves upon him, and looking to him for support.

Considerable stress may indeed be laid on this view of the family rights in inheritance lands, despite the fact that in the book of Aicill the rights of the Duthaig fine, that is, the group of the seventeen nearest kinsmen (divided into their four groups of Geilfine, Deirbhfine, Iarfine, and Indfine[2]) to succeed to the Dibad, or inheritance land of the chief, are fully expressed, and their reciprocal rights elaborately defined. The whole arrangement of the Duthaig fine, though held by

---

[1] It is certainly doubtful if the word allodial should be used, both on account of the theoretical reversion of the tribe and also on account of the payment of Bestigi by the Ceile to the chief (for even the Flath seems to have received stock from the chief), and the receipt of the Taurcrech by the Ceile, these appearing to acknowledge some dominion by the chief. Compare Sullivan, p. cxliii.

[2] *A. L. of I.* Vol. I. p. 261.

the late Sir Henry Maine to show signs of being developed
from accustomed rules of family relationship[1], is strikingly artificial, and appears to be rather a learned Brehon's elaboration
of what the rights of family succession should be, than of being
a workable system of succession, more especially in troublous
times and among a semi-barbarous community. Mr Skene
calls attention also to the passage with which these rules end,
"and the whole number of the seventeen men are then forthcoming, and if they be not, there shall be no partition but the
nearest of kin shall take[2]:" if the next of kin happened to be
powerful, judging from the record of bloodshed with which
Irish history abounds, he would have been likely to take very
practical measures to prevent the symmetrical Duthaig fine
from interfering with his title to the inheritance[3].

Dealing with these lands of inheritance there is no more
striking illustration of the unsettled state of the country than
the apparent absence of even the germ of customary tenures.
No sooner has the chief become possessed of private lands,
and allowed the settlement upon them of servile dependents,
than the gradual establishment of some base tenure similar to
that of English copyhold might have been expected; but while
the existence of this servile class is one of the most prominent
features of the early Irish society, there is no trace of any
definite rights being gained by them: on the contrary, the
large number of social outcasts, devoid of tribal rights, appears
merely to have encouraged the growth of unlimited exactions
by the chief.

The extent of the lands of inheritance would tend largely
to increase as time went on, for the chief would employ his
wealth in cattle in Saer and Daer stock loans to freemen
occupying the tribe-land, and it seems certain that the rent
payable in produce of stock and refections developed, at
least in many cases, into rent payable for the land[4]. If the

---

[1] Being apparently founded on a
principle similar to the Roman law
method as to the emancipation of sons
from the patria potestas.

[2] *Celt. Scot.* Vol. III. p. 178.

[3] The existence too of the Dergfine,

or tribe of the red-handed, composed of
those who had killed, or attempted to
kill the senior members of the fine in
order to gain their property, is an illustration of this. Sullivan, p. clxvi.

[4] See *E. Hist. of Inst.* p. 160.

Ceile fell into arrears in his produce payments, and the stock originally advanced by the chief was either destroyed by disease or carried off by raiders, the easiest mode for the chieftain to recoup himself would be to appropriate the Ceile's allotment of tribe-land as a portion of the demesne, and to reduce the Ceile to the status of a villein cultivator: nor is the shadowy right of reversion existent in the tribe likely to have afforded any sufficient barrier to such action.

There are also significant signs that a process similar to 'commendation' was not unknown as an operant factor in extinguishing the original tribal freeman. One modern writer[1] appears to carry the view of the growth of a territorial basis of society so far as to hold that the original family ties are completely merged in the land-bond; pointing out that "the possession of Deis or inheritance land which gave its owner the title of Aire, was also essential to his acquiring the privileges of the chief of a fine." Without being prepared to go quite to this length, it is certain that at the period of latest development of the Brehon Law the Ceile is found in a position in many ways assimilated to that of tenancy; the 'coyne, livery and cosherings' to which he was liable bearing a strong resemblance to the onerous incidents of feudal tenure. It was doubtless the case nevertheless that the idea of tribal possession was deeply ingrained in the Celtic race at the time when Sir John Davies commuted the Irish tenures. However far in reality the steady march of time had advanced that feudalization of the land, which in Aryan races seems always to have gone hand in hand with increase of population and the growth of the power of the chief, the idea of landlord and tenant was still strange to the Irish mind and its compulsory imposition on an unwilling people was probably a fatal mistake.

It is so evident that in the Ceile dependents of the chief is to be traced the germ of the relation of landlord and tenant, that an examination of the Brehon rules regulating the cattle loans, which brought the free tribesman into a subordinate position, is an essential preliminary to a right appreciation

[1] See Skene's *Celt. Scot.* Vol. III. p. 175.

of the nature of the Irish land system for which the English tenures were substituted. The two subtracts of the Senchus Mor in which the rules of these loans are dealt with are termed the Cain Sereath and the Cain Aigillne. From these it appears that the usual period of a Saer-stock tenancy was seven years; during this period the young of the cattle lent, the milk, and the manure, were taken by the chief. The tenant did homage, rendered help in reaping the harvest and, if required, in repairing or building the castle (*dun*) of the chief or following his banner in war. There seems to have been no fixed rule as to the amount or frequency of the services to be rendered, and here as throughout the Brehon Laws there arises the apparent difficulty of the want of a sufficient sanction, for no penalty is specifically mentioned for the non-performance of these services, save that a seeming diminution in the honour price of the tenant took place on his default[1]. After the end of the seven years the cattle became the property of the Ceile. The chief appears to have always lent the stock without security, and though no tribesman was compelled to take stock from his immediate chief yet he had no power to refuse to do so from the Ri or king[2].

These stock tenancies were terminable at will by the return of the loan. If the chief reclaimed his cattle before the end of the agreed term and the Saer Ceile expressed willingness thereupon to hold as a Daer-stock tenant he either did so (an extra amount of cattle being granted him) or the chief was liable to forfeit one-third of the original stock lent[3]. Daer-stock tenure differed in many ways from the comparatively free tenure of the Saer Ceile; the tribesman so holding received a larger amount of stock, and some security was required from him by the chief. The stock advanced was made up of two portions, one being somewhat similar to that dealt with in Saer tenancy, that is to say being proportionate to the reserved rent in kind, and the other being estimated with regard to the

---

[1] *A. L. of I.* Vol. III. Intro. p. xlix.
[2] A passage in the Cain Aigillne seems to show that this rule did not apply to Daer-stock tenants, *A. L. of I.* Vol. II. p. 223.
[3] Intro. to Vol. II. *A. L. of I.* p. xlix.

honour price[1] of the tenant. The exact amount of the rent in kind varied, and the Cain Aigillne is full of elaborate regulations as to the amount of stock proportionate to particular food-rents. One example will show the nature of these rules, " the proportionate stock of a cow with its accompaniments is thirty ' seds,' besides the returnable seds" (that is to say twenty-four cows). Thus for such a loan of twenty-four cows the food-rent would be one cow and accompaniments[2]. The severity of the Daer-stock tenure, however, lay not in the food-rent, but in the services exacted from the tenant and in such incidents of the tenure as ' refections.' Under this right of ' refection ' the Irish chieftain came with his followers and quartered himself upon the unhappy Daer-stock holder, chief and retinue living at his expense. This right was probably of ancient origin[3], and is frequently alluded to in the Cain Aigillne, but from very early times it seems to have led to grave abuses. It was the precursor of ' coyne, livery and cosherings,' forms of exaction which are bitterly denounced by Spenser and which were some of the chief causes of complaint on the part of the English settlers[4].

There are many provisions in the rules of Daer-stock tenancy tending to show that in some respects a sort of contractual relation on fairly equal terms, and with reciprocal rights and duties, was regarded as being created between the chief and the tenant[5]. These points are of interest as the after fate of the Daer-stock tenant was one of complete servitude, and it is therefore important to notice that by the rules of the Brehon Law he should have been in no small degree protected. Thus, theoretically it was possible for the Daer Ceile, without

[1] That is the price paid for injuring him.

[2] *A. L. of I.* Vol. II. p. 261.

[3] The customary entertainments given by the tenant to the chief are treated in the Corus Bescna under the head of ' human feasts '—and in them originated many abuses afterwards included under cess. *A. L. of I.* Intro. Vol. III. p. xlviii.

[4] For an account of the exaction of cess see a letter of Sir H. Sydney's to Queen Elizabeth (Sydney Papers). There is an allusion to coyne and livery in Baron Finglas' *Breviate of Ireland* (quoted in Harris' *Hibernica*) which is a proof of the light in which these exactions were regarded, it states that "they would destroy Hell if they were used in the same."

[5] See preface *A. L. of I.* Vol. II. p. lii.

the consent of the chief, to terminate the relation between them
by returning double the stock and seds, and paying a double
food-rent for the year in which they were so returned; again,
if the chief determined the tenancy without due cause he had
to forego his right to one-third of the stock and returnable
seds, and to forfeit one year's food-rent; while if the chief
insulted the tenant in withdrawing the stock the Daer holder
was allowed in addition to retain that portion representing his
honour price. Other rules provided for double food-rent becoming due if the tenant neglected his duties, while he was
excused payment in cases of poverty[1]. At the end of seven
years on the death of the chief the cattle became the property
of the tenant; while if the tenant died within the term the
chief was able to claim a submission from his co-heirs.

Before leaving the subject of lands of inheritance it is important to notice that in the later periods of the Brehon Law
this separate property appears to have been distinctly recognized, and the power of disposing of it not to have been in any
way fettered. The mode of disposal, however, presents both
curious and characteristic traits, for, unlike most archaic systems,
the consensual relations of the contracting parties rather than
the formalities observed by them in carrying out the transfer,
are looked to as constituting the binding matter. The mode of
disposing of land, moreover, seems to have presented few differences from the informal transfers of personal property. The
traces of a basis of contract in the relations of early Irish
society to the land are of much interest; not only as a great
contrast to most archaic theory, but also in view of the events
of modern history, when the application of a system of free
contract to Irish land was treated as the panacea for the accumulated evils of centuries.

The 'Mensal' lands descended by the custom of Tanistry as
the appanage of office, and here again the claims of power are
prominent. Despite the nominally elective nature of the chief-

---

[1] See *A. L. of I.* Intro. Vol. II. p. li.
and lii. Bearing in mind the curious
vitality of old-established ideas these
provisions possibly throw some light
on the keen sense of wrong felt by the
tenants in after times on capricious
evictions and evictions for non-payment of rent when caused by poverty.

taincy (which even in its latest development was elective in the
individual though hereditary in the family) *might* constituted
the pre-eminent title. The king once chosen, the Tanaist
seems always to have been selected from that branch of the
family which came next in power: for example, as pointed out
by Mr Skene " the sovereignty over the whole of Ireland fell
for several centuries into one branch of the great family called
the Northern Hy Neill and the throne was filled alternately from
two branches of it[1]." The mode of succession by Tanistry was
not a feature peculiar to the Irish tribe, for customs analogous to
it are to be traced in many other races. A prominent example of
this is pointed out by Mr Justice Field[2] in the mode of succession
to the Raj existing in many parts of India, where on the decease
of the Rajah the succession goes not to his son but to the eldest
male of the family. In this case also the same distinction is
drawn between lands which are the appanage of office and those
which are the private property of the Rajah[3]. Mensal lands
were originally intended to supply the chief with the necessary
regal state, but the principle seems to have eventually been
extended, and lands were set apart for the support of the public
officers of the community such as the Bard, Brehon, Historian,
etc. In later times the revenue of the chiefs was far more
derived from the "cuttings, cosherings and other Irish exactions,
whereby they did spoil and impoverish the people at their
pleasure[4]," than from the genuine products of their Mensal lands.

All the lands of whatever kind held by the Church are
grouped under the heading of Termon lands, so called, according to Sir John Davies, " because they were ever free from all
impositions and cuttings of the temporal lords, and had the
privilege of sanctuary." The Brehon Law recognized the claim
of the Church to tithes, firstfruits, and firstlings, under which
last head a most curious development of tenure arose: the
firstborn son was claimed as a right by the Church, and though
he obtained his equal share of the family property he held it as

---

[1] *Celt. Scot.* Vol. III. p. 150.
[2] Judge of the High Court in Bengal.
[3] Field p. 242 (note), and see also
Sir H. Maine as to similar customs

prevailing amongst the Scottish Celts.
[4] Sir John Davies' *Discoverie of
Ireland*, p. 169.

a Saer-stock tenant from the Church. It is probable that this right was not generally exacted, but it stands entirely alone as an instance of clerical power, and it is perhaps a justifiable theory that some of the Church lands were obtained as gifts in consideration of not enforcing this demand.

The Church lands were in the first place probably granted by the tribe from the common stock, and the Brehon Law recognizes to a very remarkable extent the claims of 'the tribe of the Saint' to support. The most important influence exerted by the Church on the system of land holding is that it undoubtedly did much, from more or less selfish ends, to aid free alienation of land. The Corus Bescna shows that in the case of acquisitions the Church had made great inroads on the restrictions imposed on alienation by the tribal system; and that even in allotments a successful attack had been made on the original inviolability of tribal possession, as far as regards alienation to the Church.

There is a curious similarity between the structure of the religious bodies and the primitive theory of the clan. The subdivision of the religious organization shows the same aggregate of septs, and the growth and development of each religious body appears to have exactly resembled the progress of the secular tribe. We find this assimilation to the general model even in the fragments of the tribe, the very Fuidhir tenants, and the servile groups generally, seeming instinctively to have moulded themselves in the general form, so it is perhaps not remarkable that the religious community was framed on the same lines. The relation of the Church to the tenants of ecclesiastical land is closely analogous to the dealings of the chief with the tribesman to whom he supplied stock, and the Saer Manaich and Daer Manaich holders are the exact equivalent of the Saer and Daer stock holders of the temporal community. It is far from unlikely that the extent to which lands were granted to the Church, and the way in which the original strictness of the tribal rules as to alienation were relaxed in her favour, may be traced to the fact that the possession of lands by a corporation, the existing members of which were probably allied by blood to the secular tribe, seemed a very different thing from permitting ready alienation of land to all the members of the tribe, a course which might tend to pass the lands into the keeping of a temporal enemy. The ingrained theory of tribal ownership and the absence of any real conception of tenure in the way in which the word is now used, would prevent those objections to Mortmain, which would at once occur to those trained under the feudal system, from possessing weight. The artificiality of construction shown in the similarity of the terms and ideas used in the religious clan to those used in the secular tribe must also have had the effect of strengthening the apparent unity of the two bodies, and so have lessened the antagonism to alienation. It must, however, be borne in mind that this analogy to tribal organization is not confined to the structure of the early Irish Church, but is also to be traced in many early forms of guilds and partnerships, associations which are now considered as springing solely from contract; and it has been argued that barrenness of imagination and the slow generation of ideas is responsible for the similarity, and is a distinguishing characteristic of the archaic community[1].

Passing from the Termon lands to those still held in common by the secular tribe, under a more or less modified form of the original tribal ownership, they fall naturally into two divisions:—

(1) The Common Pasturage, open to every free tribesman for the use of his cattle. In this is to be traced the origin of some of the common lands, which in later times afforded one of the subjects of contention between the landlord class and the peasant holders. Two theories of the origin of commons are advanced, termed respectively the legal and the historical[2]. The former[3] traces them to grants from the lord; while according to the latter[4] their origin is to be found in the decay of the Mark or Teutonic village community of freemen cultivating their lands in common. It is evident that neither of these theories is completely applicable to the Irish land system. The Celtic community of the Brehon Laws is found thoroughly

[1] E. Hist. of Inst. p. 229 and 232.
[2] See an article by Mr Scrutton in Law Quarterly Review 1887, also Mr Scrutton's Yorke Prize Essay on Commons and Common Fields.
[3] For an ingenious advocacy of which see Seebohm's English Village Community. See also Blackstone, Vol. II. p. 92.
[4] See Digby's History of Real Property Law, 3rd ed. p. 155 et seq.

started on an agricultural structure of open fields, and common
tillage[1], with the power of the chief greatly developed, but yet
not having attained the recognized position necessary to make
him ultimate reversionary owner of the lands, or the head of a
manorial community. For a land system in this archaic state
was suddenly substituted in the reign of James the First the
fully developed feudal system with all lands held by tenure
from the lord. Commons, therefore, which were at this time
recognized, were clearly not derived from any grant from the
lord, but existed either as the survival of the old rights of
common user by the members of the tribal community, or were
created by the English lawyers in the methodical plans on
which the various territorial settlements were based; while any
power exercised by the lord in such lands trenches on pre-
existing rights instead of extending them. This fact would not
have precluded the subsequent creation of commons by grant
had a recognized system of manorial colonies grown up. There
is no trace, however, of this development: the lowest tenants
remained fixed in a state of servile dependency; and the origin
of the common lands (the enclosure of which was in later times
so bitterly resented by the Irish peasantry as to give rise to the
forcible resistance of the 'Levellers') may therefore be ascribed
partially to the portions of land in common ownership which
were retained by the English lawyers as commons after the
destruction of the tribal system, and which were regulated and
limited by such statutes as 16 Car. I.[2] but rarely extended; and
partially to rights of user acquired in the lands which at the
time of the English settlements were left as unappropriated
waste[3].

(2)   The Arable Lands, or common tillage, which were held
in more or less permanent allotments by the members of the
tribe, the allottee being merely entitled to the usufruct. To the
allotment of such lands the possession of cattle was generally,
if not always, a condition precedent; as also to the right to

---

[1] There are passages in the Brehon
Law showing the existence of common
ploughing.

[2] c. 33.

[3] These rights in their inception
probably resembling *common pur cause
de vicinage.*

possess a habitation in the township. It was to these lands, and to the Gavelkind rules which regulated the succession to them, that the attention of the English lawyers of the reign of James the First was most directed.

If the statements of the Brehon Law, which point strongly to the existence of individual property, are compared with the statements of Sir John Davies, who seems to have considered separate property (with the exception of the chief's demesnes) as non-existent, the difference between the two views of the same system is certainly remarkable. The truth lies probably somewhere between the two, and the manner in which Sir John Davies regarded the holdings can be accounted for by the fact that his attention was doubtless most attracted by the portion of the system most foreign to English notions; nor is there any doubt that the rules of Gavelkind did apply to by far the largest portion of the Irish lands. According to these rules, as has been said, on the death of one of the sept his lands returned again into the common stock, and the "Canfinny" made a redistribution. In this distribution bastards were included, but no woman was entitled to a share. The arguments against the Irish system of Gavelkind, on the strength of which by a decision of all the judges the custom was abolished, will be treated of later under the celebrated "Case of Gavelkind": it is only necessary here to point out that far from being radically different from the Kentish custom it was in reality merely a more archaic form of the same usage, and that under it an undoubted right to the soil was vested in each member of the sept. An example of such a sept is quoted by Mr Seebohm from the State Papers of James the First; it consisted of "124 persons nearly all bearing the surname of Grame. They were divided into families, 17 of which were set down as possessed of £20 and upwards, 4 of £10 and upwards, 6 of the poorer sort, 6 of no abilities, while as dependents there were 4 servants of the name of Grame, and about a dozen irregular hangers on[1]."

Allusion has been made to the heavy exactions by the chief recognized under the Brehon Law, and much of the abuse of the

---

[1] *English Village Community*, p. 219.

English critics of the Brehon system, headed by Spenser[1], is levelled at them. Such exactions as the "eric" composition for murder, which is perhaps the one which both most attracted and biased the criticisms of the English writers, are not within the scope of this enquiry; but there were certain customs mainly in the nature of the exactions of food supply by the chief and his followers, which demand particular notice. These customs were perhaps neither very unnatural nor very serious in their inception, but they increased to an alarming extent as century after century of war rolled by, and the English colonists both adopted them as a ready means of exacting spoil from their dependents, and also it would seem increased their severity. Under the early tribal system, where the chief was regarded as the father of the community, these payments probably represented no great hardship, being exacted in a very intermittent manner and with some show of consideration; but in the hands of the degenerate English and the debased race of warlike adventurers, who in later times represented the Irish chieftaincy, they became terrible engines of oppression, and were adopted as a means of raising money even within the Colony of the Pale. The growth of these exactions has usually been ascribed to the abuse of power by the Norman settlers who, even when they had degenerated into tribal chieftains, were deemed to have been out of sympathy with the class ruled. An explanation which was offered by Dr Sullivan and adopted by the late Sir H. Maine is more probable, namely, that it was owing to the great increase of the Fuidhir tenants (a natural result of warlike times) who were in a state of servile dependence, and to whose outcast condition no tribal immunities attached.

These exactions are met with in many forms and under

---

[1] There is a marked bitterness of tone in Spenser's *View of the State of Ireland*, though it bears every trace of being in the main a truthful statement. He was himself a colonist (receiving an allotment of some 3,000 acres on the plantation of the Desmond estates) and it is not unlikely that he was embittered by the failure of his venture. A striking proof of the upheavals of society undergone on the resettlements of Irish land is found in the fact that a descendant of Spenser was ejected from this allotment under the Cromwellian settlement.

various names, but they are all of a very similar character,
consisting of a levy of food, usually exacted in primitive
fashion by the chief and his followers quartering themselves
for a more or less lengthy period on the tenant. There
appears little doubt that their origin lay in the tribal obligation to support the chief, but they certainly afterwards
developed into something closely resembling the incidents of
tenure, and were always regarded in this latter light by the
English settlers. In very early times Bonaght[1] (that is, money,
food and entertainment for his soldiers, and forage for their
horses) was exacted by the chief at pleasure, and the later development of the same custom is found in the coyne and livery[2]
alluded to in the Irish statutes as a "damnable custom," and
regarded with such fervent hatred by the English settlers[3].
Ancient exactions of a similar nature to 'Bonaght' were
'Sorohen,' 'Kernetty,' 'Gillycone,' ' Mosyorowne,' 'Gillen-
inny,' and the levy of 'South' which we find constantly
alluded to in the History of the Colony of the Pale under the
name of 'cuttings'. 'Coshery,' an exaction of provisions and
lodgings for himself and his retinue levied by the chief, is met
with again and again until the reign of James the First; and
'Refection,' a similar custom (though in its original form confined to a right of the lord to be entertained for one night),
expanded into a most heavy burden on the tenant[4]. 'Cess' was
the name given to an English exaction founded on the Irish
model, which appears to have been first established in the
reign of Edward the Second, and consisted of a tax of five marks
on every ploughland discretionally levied under the pretence of
prerogative by the chief governors of Ireland for the support of
themselves and the soldiers in garrison[5].

[1] This was of two kinds, Bonaght
Bur and Bonaght Beg, the former
being at the discretion of the lord, the
latter according to agreement. Ware,
Vol. II. p. 74.

[2] Maurice Fitz Thomas is stated to
have been the first of the English to
impose this tax, doing so in the time
of Edward II.

[3] John Cottrell was put to death
"because he had introduced and
practised many grievous, foreign and
intolerable laws."

[4] Notice also a provision of drink
termed 'satellitum poturae,' the exactions termed 'Cuddies' and 'Shragh
and Mart.' Ware, Vol. II. p. 74 and 75.

[5] In the reign of Elizabeth we find

It would be impossible to overrate the evil effects of these levies. They utterly prevented proper cultivation of the land, as the tillers of the soil saw the fruits of their labour liable to be snatched from them at any time. They diminished the estimation of all honest industry, to so great an extent that frequently the free members of the sept would not work, lest their having done so should lower them in the opinion of the chief, and cause them to be excluded from the partition of tribal lands in Gavelkind. A further expansion of the same idea being seen in the class of descendants of a chief, who, when prevented from living by a system of wholesale plunder, would rather perish miserably than stoop to what they deemed menial pursuits. Special attention is drawn to these exactions from the fact that they were the moral justification advanced for the complete substitution of English tenures for the Brehon system. That, as has been stated, they constituted a most crying evil is doubtless true, but perhaps it is often forgotten that the English law which was substituted for them was neither a very enlightened nor a very humane institution : for example, the eric fine is certainly repugnant to notions of right, and is palpably open to abuse in the hands of the wealthy and unscrupulous[1], but the penal code substituted for it would nowadays be considered a flagrant evil. It is almost certain also that there was a distinction between the free tenant and the fuidhir settled on the waste as regards the liability to the exactions of food levies, and that the rights of the former have often been confused with the servile liabilities of the latter.

When dealing with the substitution of the English for the Brehon Law one is struck with the entire variance which the two systems seem to represent, and it is hard to realize that they are in reality merely different stages of development of kindred institutions, and that " the germs of feudalism lay deep in the more ancient Irish social structure." The Brehon Laws certainly show a system to which the notion of feudal ownership is completely foreign ; but, as has been shown, these primitive tribal conceptions had been greatly modified, and the pre-

a protest against the increase of this   [1] *E. Hist. of Inst.* p. 170.
tax. See Ware, Vol. II. p. 77.

eminent power of the chief would seem to have been in some
respects a greater evil than the summary feudalization of the
land. Spenser, whose account, if prejudiced, is yet seldom
really inaccurate, states that the chiefs " use most shamefully
to racke their tenants, laying upon them coin and livery at
pleasure, and exacting of them besides their covenants what he
pleaseth[1]," and Sir John Davies stated that " the lord was an
absolute tyrant and the tenant a very slave[2]."

---

[1] Spenser, p. 57.   [2] Sir J. Davies' *Discoverie*, p. 179.

CHAPTER III.

THE COLONY OF THE PALE

(FROM HENRY II. TO HENRY VII.).

THE influence of the more advanced civilization of foreign nations was little felt by the early Irish laws and institutions; and the various predatory incursions, which in early times ravaged the coasts of Ireland, left no permanent mark on the tribal system of land-holding, the Norse land system indeed differing but little from the Irish. From the time of Henry the Second of England, however, a new feature was introduced by the appearance of feudal tenures. It is true that though nominally spread all over the country it was only—until the time of Elizabeth—within a comparatively limited area that these tenures for any length of time held sway; still from the latter part of the twelfth century, some portion of the land of Ireland was always so held. The two systems of land-holding, Brehon and feudal, existed side by side; but save where the latter had been imposed by force of arms, it gained no converts from the native race, and failed to alter their ideas of the relation of the occupier to the land. On the other hand the Brehon Law secured many adherents from among the English invaders. The causes of this were various. As Mr Froude observes, "the Irish Celts possess on their own soil a power greater than any known family of mankind of assimilating those who venture among them to their own image[1]," and the intermarriages of the English settlers[2] with the native popu-

---

[1] *The English in Ireland*, Vol. I. p. 21.

[2] Strongbow married Eva, the daughter of Dermot Mac Murrough, and his followers also largely contracted Irish marriages.

lation created a class of Anglo-Irish who, born in the country
and imbued with the native ideas, were galled by the restrictions of the feudal tenures by which their lands were
held[1]. The customs of Gavelkind and Tanistry also attracted
the younger sons and bastards, whom the strict rules of feudal
descent excluded from a share in the inheritance[2]. In result,
until the time of James the First, save in the Colony of the
Pale[3], the feudal tenures did not hold, and in no way modified
the Brehon rules which were observed in the rest of Ireland.

It was pointed out by the late Sir Henry Maine[4] that to
the existence of the English Colony, we are indebted for much
of the archaic nature of the Brehon Law being preserved to
so late a date in history as it was. The Colony " acting as a
running sore " prevented the internal disturbances of Ireland
from self-adjustment by the natural process of the merger of
all lesser states in one great master kingdom. Had such
arisen it would have established a centralized government,
and thus by endowing the Brehon Code with the force of more
certain judicial sanctions would have greatly modified the
loosely administered and in many cases conflicting laws, and
even in the end have changed the theory of land-holding by
the simple process of development.

The English invasion of Ireland took place towards the
latter part of the reign of Henry the Second (though it is
evident by the Bull obtained from Adrian the Fourth in 1155[5]

---

[1] There is ample proof that they
regarded with even more dislike than
did the native Irish, the aids, reliefs,
&c. of the feudal tenures.

[2] Primogeniture, however, though
by this time fairly established as a
characteristic of the feudal system, was
not a feature of the early feud, which
descended to all the sons equally, while
from Glanville we know that as late as
Henry II. land held in socage frequently
descended to all the sons equally.

[3] The term 'Colony of the Pale'
arose from the provision of Poyning's
law (1494) which enjoined on the
English colony the maintenance of

a double ditch, six feet high 'on the
side which meared next to the Irish-
man' (see Field, p. 249). In the earlier
periods of English rule the district
occupied by the English was termed
'the land of Ireland.'

[4] E. Hist. of Inst., pp. 54 and 55.

[5] This Bull reserved a payment of
Peter's pence to Rome, and was in
fact a bold attempt to make Ireland
a spiritual fee—it was confirmed by
Alexander III. The Papal claim of
right to make this grant was based on
the forged donation of Constantine,
which gave all islands to the see of
Rome.

that Henry had early[1] meditated a descent upon that country)
when, urged by the tempting bribes offered by Dermot Mac
Murrough to those who would assist him to recover the
kingship of Leinster, an expedition of Norman and Welsh
adventurers landed in Ireland in May, 1169[2]. The command
of this expedition was ultimately assumed by Richard de Clare,
Earl of Pembroke, better known as Strongbow, who landed
near Waterford with some 1200 men and 200 knights on the
eve of St Bartholomew, 1170. Besides many small tribes
there were at this time five principal sovereignties in Ireland,
Munster, Leinster, Meath, Ulster, and Connaught, the leader
of the most powerful of these being termed monarch of Ireland,
and holding Meath as an appanage of office. This post was
then occupied by Roderic O'Connor, king of Connaught,
against whom the efforts of the English expedition were
directed. Strongbow was successful in gaining the more or
less complete possession of Dublin, Meath, Leinster, and Waterford as far as Dungarvan; but the expedition, which at first
had the countenance of the English king, ere long incurred
his displeasure. Strongbow, finding his supplies from England
cut off, and his precarious position in Ireland rendered practically untenable, offered to Henry the lands he had won[3].
After some delay, and after an interview had taken place at
Gloucester between the Earl and the King, Henry accepted
the surrender of Dublin and all other ports and fortresses
then (or to be) conquered in Ireland, and granted to the Earl

---

[1] Henry is sometimes thought to
have originally intended Ireland for
his brother William, for whom no
provision had been made by their late
father (see Moore's *Hist. of Ireland*,
Vol. II. p. 205). William the Conqueror had planned the conquest of
Ireland, William Rufus had had similar designs. See Pearson, p. 520 quoting A. S. Chron. and Girald. Camb.

[2] This date is sometimes given as
1170.

[3] Strongbow first despatched Ray-
mond Le Gros to Henry in Normandy

with the following letter, "My sovereign lord, I came into this land, and
(if I remember aright) with your permission, for the purpose of restoring
your liegeman Dermot Mac Murrough,
and whatsoever the favour of fortune
has bestowed upon me, whether from
his patrimony or from any other
source, as to your generous munifi-
cence I owe it all, so shall it all return
to you, and be placed at the disposal
of your absolute will and pleasure.
See Moore, Vol. II. p. 235.

and his heirs for ever all his other acquisitions, to be held
as fiefs of the English crown. From this period dates the
authority of the English monarchs over Ireland, and the existence of the feudal tenures in that country.

In October 1171[1], Henry himself landed in Ireland with
500 knights and about 4000 men; the chief event of his stay
of importance as affecting the land law of Ireland being the
holding of a Curia Regis at Lismore[2], at which Council it is
stated that the laws of England were accepted under oath by
those present[3]. It is probably incorrect, however, to imagine
that the English law was ever intended to apply to the mass
of native Irish; for at the Synod of Cashel the Irish clergy
were specially exempted from the payment of the eric fine[4],
and from coyne and coshering—provisions which would be
meaningless unless such incidents of the Irish land system
had been contemplated as remaining in force amongst the
native race[5]. In support of this view it is noticeable that
when a confirmatory grant of the laws and customs of England
was given by John, and again by Henry the Third, it was
confined to such of the Irish as became liege subjects; also
there are large numbers of Royal grants of naturalization made
upon petition to the offspring of Anglo-Irish marriages, giving
them the benefit of the English laws and franchises[6]. Henry's

---

[1] This date is often stated to be Oct.
1172, but see Dr O'Connor's criticisms
on Leland, *Rer. Hib. scrip.*, tom. II.
cxv.; see also Lord Lyttelton's *Life of
Henry II.*, Field, p. 244. Girald. Camb.
gives date as 1172.

[2] Whatever laws were enacted at this
time are lost, but we find an allusion
to one of the statutes passed by Henry
in 2 Rich. III. c. 8.

[3] "Sed rex pater, antequam ab Hy-
bernia rediret, apud Lissemor conci-
lium congregavit, ubi leges Angliae ab
omnibus sunt gratanter acceptae, et,
juratoria cautione praestita confirma-
tae." Matth. Paris. "Historia An-
glorum." Rolls Series, Vol. I. p. 371.

[4] "That when earick or composition

is made among the lay people, for any
murther, that no person of the clergy
(though he be kin to any of the parties)
shall contribute anything thereto, but
as they be guiltless from the murther,
so shall they be free from payment of
mony, for any such earick or release
for the same." See Cox's *History of
Ireland*, p. 23, and Giraldus Cambren-
sis. Rolls Series, Vol. v. ch. 35, p.
281.

[5] Thomas Moore's *History of Ireland*, Vol. II. pp. 258, 259.

[6] See Warner's *History of Ireland*,
p. 93, and Moore, Vol. II. p. 332 (note),
says, "among the records of the Irish
Rolls office are many of these licenses
granted to particular Irish to use the

object was not so much to regulate the customs and manner of the minor and native Irish holdings, as to obtain a public ratification of his feudal lordship from the English settler barons, and from the more important Irish chieftains. Nevertheless all the laws enacted by him when in Ireland followed the feudal polity, and the estates he granted were in consideration of homage, fealty, and military or honorary service; the grantees under tenures then created being tenants in capite, examples being the tenure on which Strongbow received the principality of Leinster, and Hugh de Lacy the seigniory of Meath[1].

It should be remembered that the English feudal system of this date was a more complete engine of monarchical power than continental feudalism, which possessed a weak point in the absence of immediate relation between the tenant of a mesne lord and the feudal sovereign. William, on the conquest of England, utilized the existence of the 'trinoda necessitas' as a lever for remedying this blot[2], and by the time of Henry the Second the doctrine that where land was held of a mesne lord, the service was due to the king, was firmly established; the form of homage adopted after the Conquest to create the feudal tie between a mesne lord and his tenant always containing a saving of the allegiance due to the king. The system in Ireland was, however, in many cases different[3]. The large

English laws, some of them being Irish women whose husbands were English." Attention is also called to the careful exclusion of the native Irish as a mass from English privileges. A grant is quoted of English privileges to two Irishmen, given in the Close Roll 37 Henry III., where the writ especially states that this favour was granted them "notwithstanding that they were Irish," Vol. III. p. 22. Notice also two records, viz. 2 Ed. III. Claus. Membr. 17, and 28 Ed. III. quoted in the 'Case of Tanistry.' Davies' Reports, p. 103.

[1] Meath, as the former appanage of Irish Royalty, had passed to the English crown, and by this grant Hugh de Lacy obtained about 800,000 acres, held by the tenure of fifty knights' service. The Baronial Courts held within this area eventually became so powerful that they were suppressed as interfering with the rights of the crown, see Moore's *History of Ireland*. This large grant was evidently made with a view to counterbalancing the power of Strongbow.

[2] Notice the oath at Sarum, A.D. 1086.

[3] For example in the cases of Strongbow and de Lacy, and later in the cases of the Butlers and Geraldines.

grants which Henry made were grants which carried also the privileges of a county Palatine[1], and gave to the grantee the right of civil and criminal jurisdiction independent of the crown[2]. The lord of such a fee could enfeoff tenants to hold of himself, escheats for treason accrued to him instead of to the crown, and the king's process ranged only in the church lands[3].

Henry did not assume the title of king of Ireland, but seems to have been satisfied with being acknowledged a sort of 'paramount power[4].' It has been asserted, and is not unlikely, that much of the readiness with which the Irish chieftains submitted to him was due to the fact that they merely understood the feudal bond as binding them to a general support of the king by military service, and were in complete ignorance of the change in the title to their lands which the subtle and intricate system of the Norman lawyers deduced from the apparently simple ceremony of homage and fealty. Mr Pearson says " From the English point of view, the kings of England were henceforth lords-paramount of Ireland, with the fee of the soil vested in them, and all Irish princes in future were no more than tenants-in-chief. From the Irish point of view, the English kings were nothing more than military suzerains in the districts outside the Pale[5]."

Roderic O'Connor, though crippled in power by the conquests of Strongbow and reduced to treat for peace, was still far from conquered at the time when the English king visited Ireland, and it is probable that steps would have been taken to reduce him to subjection had not the investigation then pending into the death of Becket forced Henry to return home in April 1172[6]. Ireland was then, in name at least, completely conquered,

---

[1] In the proceedings of the Irish Parliament in 1467 among the unprinted statutes is one enacting that the Palatine liberty of Meath, despite its merger in the crown by inheritance, should continue.

[2] Hallam's *Const. Hist.*, Vol. III. chapter 18, p. 347.

[3] But by the statute of Kilkenny the king's sheriffs were entitled to enter all franchises for the apprehension of felons or traitors.

[4] It is noticeable that even the Leinster provinces of Strongbow, though acquired in right of his wife, were surrendered and reconveyed in feudal form.

[5] *Hist. of Eng. during Early and Middle Ages*, Vol. I. p. 531.

[6] Whence it is said he sent a 'modus

Ulster alone being admittedly unsubdued. In 1175 a treaty was concluded at Windsor between Henry and the emissaries of Roderic, by which Roderic, in consideration of having done homage and undertaking an annual tribute for himself and the Irish at large of one merchantable hide for every tenth head of cattle killed in Ireland outside the English provinces, was to hold his lands peaceably, as a king under Henry, and to have dominion over all Ireland save the then English possessions of Dublin, Meath, Leinster and Waterford[1], provided he remained faithful and preserved his covenants[2]. If Roderic regarded this treaty but lightly the English king also seems not to have felt in the least fettered by it, and it is probable that he had from the first only regarded it as another means of asserting his paramount suzerainty over the whole of Ireland: for despite its provisions "all Ireland was by Henry the Second cantonized amongst ten of the English nation, and though they did not gain possession of one-third of the kingdom, yet in title they were owners and lords of all, as nothing was left to be granted to the natives[3]."

The policy of Henry is evident; he intended that the feudal grantees should subdue this turbulent kingdom, and in serving their own ends establish also the dominion of the English kings over the whole of Ireland. One cannot but wonder that the far-sighted scheme was not fulfilled in history. That the descendants of the chivalry, which only a hundred years before

tenendi Parliamenta' to Ireland, but the authority and antiquity of this document cannot be maintained despite the championship of it by Sir Edward Coke.

[1] Waterford that is to say as far as Dungarvan.

[2] Quod Rex Angliae concedit praedicto Roderico, Ligeo homini suo Regnum Conaciae, quamdiu ei fideliter serviet, ut sit Rex sub eo, paratus ad servitium suum, sicut homo suus .. ut teneat terram suam ita bene, .. in pace, sicut tenuit, antequam Dominus Rex Angliae intravit Hiberniam reddendo

ei tributum : totam illam terram .. habitatores terrae habeat sub se ; .. Justitiae ut tributum Regi Angliae integre persolvant, per manum ejus sua jura sibi conservent, .. illi qui modo tenent, teneant in pace, quamdiu manserint in fidelitate Regis Angliae, .. fideliter .. integre persolverint tributum, .. alia jura sua quae ei debent, per manum Regis Conaciae, salvo in omnibus jure .. honore Domini Regis Angliae .. suo, etc. etc.—Cox's *Hist. of I.* page 29.

[3] Sir John Davies' *Discoverie*, p. 137,—and see Field, p. 244, 245.

rode rough-shod over Saxon England, and a century and a half
before that wrested Normandy from "Frank Noblesse and
Romanesque provincials," carving so goodly a heritage with the
sword, should have failed for centuries to subdue an uncivilized
people, is in many ways remarkable. The Irish, despite their
valour, were most contemptible adversaries to Norman disci-
pline, and that civilization should have failed to follow the
victorious banner is a curious problem. Stranger still is it to
find that as time went on not only did the English power in
Ireland wane, and the limits of the Colony of the Pale become
more and more contracted, but also that the glamour of the
Celt was over all the land; that proud de Burgh and courtly
Geraldine had become mere tribal chieftains[1]; that the Butlers
ruled but as half civilized petty kings; and that the descendants
of the frugal, scholarly, priest-army of the Conqueror William
had sunk to lives of debauchery and rapine. The children of a
race who had written their laws in blood on the English statute
book threw off the shackles of the system their ancestors had so
laboriously welded, and assimilated themselves to the social
condition and primitive land system of the Brehon Law to such
an extent that the law of England was never "properly applied
unto the Irish nation as of a purposed plot of government[2]"
until James the First.

In May 1177 Henry (having obtained a permissive Bull
from Pope Alexander the Third) in Council at Oxford constituted John, a child of eleven, king of Ireland[3]; the Legate
Vivianus having shortly before this held a Synod at Dublin in
which he published the king's title. The Prince, however, is
always termed merely Lord of Ireland and Earl of Moreton. The

---

[1] *Land System of Ireland*, O'Connor
Morris, *L. Q. R.* 1887, p. 137.

[2] Spenser's *View and perfect Discovery of Ireland*, edition 1633, p. 10.

[3] This donation of Ireland to John
has given rise to many controversies
(1) as to whether it created Ireland a
separate kingdom from England, (2)
as to whether it prevented the laws of
England being binding on Ireland.

The matter was mooted before the
English judges in the decision on the
precedent of the Staple Act (2 Hen.
VI.). Chief Justice Coke, Sir J. Davies
and Molyneux have all treated at
length of the matter, and reference
should be made to Sir J. Davies'
speech in 1613 when Speaker of the
Irish House of Commons. See Moore,
Vol. II. p. 329.

feudal grants before made by Henry were confirmed with alterations by new charters under which the lands were generally held from John instead of from the king[1]. These grants, however, are very inconsistent, Henry's opinion of the wisdom of the step he had taken in constituting John king of Ireland seeming to vary from time to time. Frequently the appointment appears to have been altogether disregarded: there are grants by Henry, subsequent to the Council at Oxford, in which lands are granted to be held of himself alone and his heirs, while others grant by tenure from him and John and their heirs[2]. Grants of fiefs not formerly existing were also made at this time[3] (many of which were never more than nominal, the grantees failing to reduce them to subjection), and the policy of Henry for the subjection of the land was followed by his grantees who largely subinfeudated their possessions.

In 1185 John, then only nineteen years of age, landed at Waterford with a considerable force. His stay, which might have ended in the complete subjection of the Irish, was really the commencement of that decay of the English power which left the Colony of the Pale at the close of the fifteenth century possessed of merely a strip of land round Dublin. The offence given by the Prince and his followers to the Irish tributary chiefs, the impolitic resumption of the royal demesnes, and the unjust and shameful expedition of Philip of Worcester into Ulster, sowed the seeds of wide-spread revolt and successful retaliation; whilst the recall of John and the appointment of de Courcy as governor came too late to be availing. The succession of Richard the First to the English crown did not interfere with the nominal lordship or kingship of John over Ireland, and for the next hundred years the history of this unhappy country is a record of bloodshed and rapine. The English settlers strove by force to gain possession of the broad lands so glibly granted them, and "they built castles and made freeholds but no tenures or services were reserved to the crown[4];" while both the Irish chieftains and English

---

[1] e.g. The new grant of Meath to Hugh de Lacy.

[2] See Moore, Vol. II. p. 330.

[3] e.g. The grant of Limerick or North Munster.

[4] See Field, p. 245.

lords warred amongst themselves as well as against one another. As still further extending the titular claims of the English to the Irish soil a surrender should be noticed in 1205 by Cathal, son of Roderic, to John. This arrangement finally abandoned the violated treaty of Windsor, delivered to the English crown two-thirds of Connaught, and acknowledged John's lordship over the remainder by the annual payment of one hundred marks[1]. In 1210 John, this time in the full dignity of King of England, but under the ban of excommunication, again visited Ireland, and received the homage of many Irish princes and settler barons. To this date is ascribed the division of the English provinces into shires and counties; and it is also stated that an abstract of the laws and customs of England was placed in the Exchequer at Dublin. An allusion to this gift of the English laws is contained in the writ of 11 Hen. III.[2], but as has been before stated neither of these grants seems to have had any real application to the native Irish[3]. The visit of John, as indeed the whole of his reign, advanced but little the summary feudalization of the main body of Ireland. Within the English colony, however, the feudal system was fully followed, at any rate in its most onerous incidents, for there are many writs of this reign extant demanding 'consilium et auxilium[4]'.

The reign of Henry the Third of England produced also but little benefit; the Irish Charter proved a worthless gift, and was never intended to reach the case of the native race. A variety of new grants in feudal form[5] are noticeable, chief among which is that of the whole of Connaught to Richard

---

[1] John was allowed, it would seem, to choose his portions from the best of the province. See letter to Meiler Fitz-Henry, quoted by Leland, Vol. I. p. 175.

[2] See Cox, p. 51, where the writ of Henry III. is quoted.

[3] See ante, p. 43.

[4] See Moore. In the Incorporation Charter of Dublin given in 1192, burgage tenure is established. The first case of legal action against a tenant by a landlord within the Pale seems to be under Stat. West. 2nd (13 Edw. I.) which gave a right to a writ of cessavit against the tenant for two years' default in the reserved services. See Sigerson, pp. 15, 16 (note).

[5] Henry III. made his son Edward 'lord of Ireland,' and a writ (*Rot. Pat.* 40 Hen. III. m. 12) authorised the Prince's seal as the great seal of Ireland, see *Constitution of England and Ireland*, by Sir W. Betham, p. 254.

de Burgh, in utter defiance of John's re-grant to Cathal on his
surrender of that province which has been alluded to before[1].
The conflicting titles[2] to the Irish provinces at this time
were of themselves sufficient to stir up war, independent of
the national animosities involved; and murder, massacre, and
treachery form the staple of the history of this period. In
1272, a century from the installation of the English power in
Ireland, a petition was presented to Edward the First asking
for the extension to the Irish of the laws and customs of
England. The petitioners were most likely the inhabitants
of the districts adjoining the Colony, and the memorial does
not seem to have been considered until 1280, or to have led
to any important result, but it is a significant proof of the
failure of English civilization to extend outside the limits of
the Pale[3].

Maddened by oppression and outrage[4] the native race
sought in 1315 the assistance of Bruce to destroy the English
dominion, but upon the failure of his expedition they merely
found themselves in worse case than before, and fresh exactions
and severities were heaped upon 'the mere Irish.' Slowly
but surely, however, the Celtic race had been absorbing to

[1] See ante, p. 49.

[2] As late as 1220 the Pope in sending letters to Connaught, Ulster and
Munster, addressed the *kings* of Connaught, Cork, Limerick and Ulster.
See *Church History of Ireland*, S. Ma-
lone.

[3] Attention was called by Sir W.
Betham to the fact that the size of
the Placita Rolls of the Courts are an
indication by which the extent of
English law and power at different
times may be judged. During the
reigns of Henry III. and Edward I.,
Edward II. and Edward III. they are
large and well-written, "pleas and as-
sizes were held by the justices itinerant
in most parts of Ireland, and the plead-
ings exhibit an exact sequence and all
regularity of form and precedent."
After these reigns they steadily decrease

"until the term rolls, from the portly
size of from 60 to 90 membranes, for
the proceedings of each, are shrunk
to four." *Constitution of England and
Ireland*, p. 350.

[4] How really great were the wrongs
of the Irish people is shown by the
statement of their case forwarded to
the Pope about this time, by O'Neil,
prince of Tyrone, which appears to be
no exaggerated catalogue of injustice
and crime; and by the record cited by
Sir John Davies (*Discoverie*, p. 109),
4 Edw. II. where a murderer's defence
reads " bene cognovit quod prædictum
Johannem interfecit; dicit tamen quod
per ejus interjectionem feloniam com-
mittere non noluit, quia dicet quod
prædictus Johannes fuit purus Hi-
bernicus."

itself and incorporating in its being the descendants of the proud Norman settler barons. Severed from England and tied to the land of their adoption, the subtle influence of the soil and the alteration in the blood by admixture of race, had their natural effect. The amalgamation was aided, moreover, by the wild anarchy of the land, for in times when every man's hand was against his brother, an English lord of an Irish fief must have owed all his chances not only of supremacy but of actual existence to the loyalty to his banner of his Irish dependents; and while "to the Irish kern it mattered little whether his chief was a Geraldine or an O'Connor; it mattered much whether he was to be ruled under the imported laws of the stranger or by the customs and traditions of his own people.... The baron and his Irish retainers found the relations between them grow easy when the customs of the country were allowed to stand[1]." So, by a strange irony of fate, the very men and means designed for the subjugation of the native system endowed it with a stubborn vitality quite foreign to its natural character.

The defection of the English-born subjects of the crown was not tamely countenanced by either the home government or the English Colony, and in 1341 the policy of the English king was specially directed towards breaking the power and wealth of these descendants of the first Anglo-Norman conquerors of Ireland. The first step taken was "a general resumption of all the lands, liberties, seigniories, and jurisdictions that had been granted in Ireland not only by Edward the Third himself but also by his father[2]." Next followed in 1342 the removal of the Anglo-Irish from offices under the crown[3]; and in 1355 came a series of ordinances forbidding intermarriages betwixt English and Irish, and rendering illegal the practice of fostering[4] which was largely carried on.

---

[1] *English in Ireland*, Froude, Vol. i. p. 24.

[2] Moore, Vol. iii. p. 95.

[3] Close Roll, 15 Edw. III. In the reign of Edw. III. also was passed an "Ordinatio pro statu terrae Hiberniae," 31 Edw. III. st. 4, to amend the administration of justice in Ireland.

[4] This practice of fostering was of great antiquity, and Dr Whitley Stokes, in the *Tripartite Life of St Patrick*, Vol. i. p. clxix, says, "The relations of fosterer and fosterling seem

Some doubt has been expressed as to the way in which English statutes were made to apply to Ireland. It is customary to find in the Irish enactments allusions to the English statutes as though without any formality they were as a matter of course part of the law of Ireland: it is most likely that they were introduced by the simple process of sending them over under the great seal, the methods of legislation being at this date arbitrary in the extreme[1].

Gradually but surely as time went on the power of the Celtic customs made head against the English laws, and the Anglo-Irish rulers became more and more synonymous with the native race. At length in 1367 was passed the memorable Act known as the Statute of Kilkenny, by which a determined effort was made, on the part of those settlers and colonists who were still loyal to the English rule, to stem the tide of Celtic influence[2]. By this statute it was made treason for one of English birth or blood to accept or rule by the Brehon Law; and to intermarry, or to permit the fosterage of children[3] with the Irish: whilst the penalty of forfeiture was attached to those who adopted the names, tongue, or manners of the mere Irish. The efforts of civilization to reclaim her errant children came, however, too late, and from this time the legislation of the English colony is occupied more in repeated and futile attempts at the repression of the alien and degenerate English

in Ireland to have been of almost more importance than those of parent and child;" he mentions that there was frequently a plurality of fosterers, instancing Cormac, the son of Euda, who had four, and the curious question addressed to St Patrick as to whether 'God's son had many foster fathers' (si filium ejus nutrierunt multi).

[1] See Reeve's *History of the English Law*, Vol. II. p. 249, 250.

[2] How strong this influence had become is shown by the following extract. "Et ore plusors Engleis de la dit terre guepissant la lang, gis, monture, leys, usages. Engleis vivent et se governent as Maniers, guise, et lang des Irrois enemies, et auxaint ownt fait divers mariages et aliaunces enter eux et les Irrois enemyes" (quoted by Sigerson from "Tracts relating to Ireland," Irish Archæological Society). This statute was renewed by every Parliament until 1452.

[3] The subject of fosterage as dealt with in the Brehon Law will be found in the 'Cain Iarrath,' one of the subtracts of the Senchus Mor. It presents a glimpse of the social life of the Irish worthy of much attention,—for an able resumé see the introduction to the second volume of the *Ancient Laws of Ireland*.

than in a struggle against the purely native race. When Richard the Second in 1394 came over to Ireland, the force at his command, it is true, for a time brought the lapsed chiefs again to their allegiance, but the revival of English authority was only temporary. The absenteeism of many of the loyal lords prevented any possibility of the retention of power over the Anglo-Irish chieftains, and the prohibition of absenteeism under pain of forfeiture does not appear to have efficaciously grappled with the difficulty. The circle of the English colony grew steadily less, and in the reign of Henry the Fourth there are significant proofs of the decreased power of the Pale and the formidable encroachments upon it by the Irish, in the licenses given to particular colonists to war with "the enemy." In addition there are licenses to trade, and (despite the Statute of Kilkenny) to intermarry and to enter into gossipred and fosterage with the Irish, which are manifestly concessions to the exigencies of circumstances[1]; a fact further shown by the payment of 'black rent' by the English authorities to buy off the hostility of neighbouring chieftains. Towards the end of this reign it was admitted in Parliament by the Speaker of the English House of Commons that the greater part of Ireland had been 'conquered' by the natives[2]; and the conquests of Henry the Fifth in France prevented a great military genius from employing in the subjugation of what was nominally his own kingdom, the army with which for a time France was 're-duced to an English province[3].'

---

[1] Instances of these licenses are quoted by Moore, Vol. III. pp. 148, 149 :—

(1) To make war..."Rex, pro eo quod maneria et possessiones Cornelii Episcopi in Lym. in frontura marchiarum inter Hibernicos inimicos et Anglicos rebelles sita sunt, concessit ei, tenentibus et serventibus suis quod ipsi cum dictis Hibernicis, etc. tractare possent." Pat. Roll 10 Hen. IV.

(2) For fosterage..."Rex, pro servicio, licentiam dedit Willielmo filio Henric. Betagh quod ipse Elizam filiam suam cuidam Odoni Oraylly Hibernico dare

possit ad nutriendum." Pat. Roll 7 Hen. IV.

[2] See Lingard's *Hist. of Eng.*, Vol. II. p. 320.

[3] A military expedition round the borders of the Pale was indeed carried out with success during this reign by Sir John Talbot, but it was productive of no lasting effect and is mainly noticeable from the fact that the ill-paid soldiery levied 'coyne and livery' on the inhabitants of the Colony; a curious instance of the vitality of the Irish customs.

The inattention displayed by the conqueror of Agincourt to the needs of Ireland was not caused by any want of energy on the part of the English colony there in proclaiming their grievances. In the Close Roll of 9 Henry V, is a most lengthy petition[1] for redress of their wrongs, which amongst other points complains to the king that "his poor lieges are distressed, and his land, for the greater part, wasted and destroyed by the Irish enemies and English rebels, as well by their continual wars on his said lieges in each country of his said land, as by divers extortions, oppressions, non-payments and evil coignes by divers lieutenants......and by default of due execution of his laws." Henry the Fifth, however, was totally engrossed by continental conquest, and no heed seems to have been paid to the representations from Ireland. On his death the guardians of Henry the Sixth had more important matters to deal with at home, and the result of this neglect was soon apparent. About this time it was stated "yr is not left in the nethir parties of the counties of Dyvelin (Dublin), Mith (Meath), Loueth and Kildare, that yoynin to gadyr, oute of the subjection of the saide enemyes and rebels scarisly xxx miles in lengthe, and xx in brede ther, as a man may surely ride other go, to answerre to the Kynge's writtes[2]."

---

[1] Quoted in full by Sir W. Betham, *The Constitution of England and Ireland*, pp. 335—350.

[2] Sigerson, p. 21: see also two representations of the state of Ireland sent to Hen. VI. which are in the Close Roll 7 Hen. VI. and 14 Hen. VI. respectively, both are quoted by Betham, pp. 353—365.

CHAPTER IV.

The Colony of the Pale

(From Henry VII. to James I.).

When the House of Tudor ascended the English throne a marked change came over the relations of England to Ireland. Following out in succession that bent for the establishment of law and order which was the distinguishing characteristic of these powerful sovereigns, a determined effort was made to reduce to subjection the turbulent country. Henry the Seventh was not firmly enough seated on the English throne to accomplish much, but after the defeat of the Anglo-Irish expedition in favour of Simnel at Stoke he sent Sir Richard Edgecombe in 1488 to exact new oaths of allegiance from the Irish feudatories[1]. It is curious, therefore, to note that Henry the Seventh seems to have considered that the policy of Henry the Second as to the subjection of Ireland by the agency of feudal lords, was the best plan of introducing order into the country ; whereas in England his efforts were directed to breaking the power of the barons. After the Warbeck plots the famous Statute of Drogheda termed 'Poyning's Law[2]' was passed, which restricted the holding of Parliaments in Ireland save when the causes and considerations of Acts intended to be passed had been approved by the English King and Council[3]. It was to the provision of this law respecting the maintenance of a frontier fortification by the English settlement that the term 'Colony of the Pale' is due. Acts of this date also revive the Statute of Kilkenny[4]; contain many provisions for

---

[1] Field, p. 248.

[2] Passed at Drogheda in November, 1494, called after Sir Edward Poyning,

then sent into Ireland as deputy.

[3] 10 Henry VII. c. 4 (Irish).

[4] Ib. c. 8 (Irish).

the better protection of the Marches[1]; and deal with the heavy
exactions by the lords[2], a very necessary step, for "doomed to
suffer by the peculiar oppressions of both countries, Ireland
was harassed not only by her own ancient exactions, coyne
and livery, but also by the English mode of extortion, pur-
veyance[3]." Eventually Henry the Seventh seems to have
abandoned his original plan of ruling by means of the
Anglo-Irish barons, for, with a view to crushing their power,
an Act was passed for the resumption of the greater part of
the crown grants made since the time of Edward the Second[4].
It is important to bear in mind that though when first made
laws practically affected merely the Colony of the Pale, yet
as the power of the crown extended over Ireland so did the
statute law.

On the accession of Henry the Eighth a policy, at once
more extended in its aims and more vigorous in its execution
than had before characterized the English relations with Ireland, was entered upon. This as first carried out was free
from the severity which it afterwards developed[5]. Still following the idea of obtaining subjection by means of crown
feudatories Henry strove to resuscitate the system of Anglo-
Irish lords, and to assimilate the native Irish Princes to the
same model. The desire to vest large estates in the grantees
of the crown evidently aimed at the hold which would be
thus obtained upon such grantees by the forfeiture to which
their estates would become liable in case of treason; and it
was doubtless considered that the antagonism of interest
created between the feudal grantee and tribal usage would
lead to the total overthrow of the popular system[6]. To the
ever recurrent overthrow of schemes which the English, to do
them justice, considered great reforms, must be ascribed much

[1] 10 Henry VII. c. 10 (Irish).

[2] Ib. c. 18 (Irish).

[3] Moore, Vol. III. p. 221. By 10
Hen. VII. c. 22 all the statutes made
in England relating to the public weal
were made good and effectual also
as regards Ireland.

[4] Cox, p. 189. Henry however par-

doned most of the great men who had
been engaged in the Warbeck Plot,
and the Liberties and Charter of
Youghal were restored and confirmed.
Cox, p. 192.

[5] O'Connor Morris, L. Q. Review,
1887, p. 138.

[6] See Intro. A. L. of I. Vol. III.

of the bitterness of feeling with which Irish customs were regarded.

A report prepared for Henry the Eighth in 1515[1] gives a graphic description of the state of Ireland at that time; after prefacing that "Ther byn more than 60 countryes, called Regyons, in Ireland, inhabytyd with the Kinges Irish enymyes; some region as bygge as a shyre, some more, some lesse, unto a lytyll; some as bygge as halffe a shyre and some a lytyll lesse; where reygneith more than 60 chyef Capytaynes wherof some callyth themselffes Kynges,......that lyveyth onely by the swerde, and obeyeth to no other temperall person, but onely to himself that is stronge; and every of the said Capytaynes makeyth warre and peace for hymself, and holdeith by swerde, and hath imperiall jurysdyction within his rome, and obeyeth to noo other person, Englyshe ne Iryshe, except only to suche persones, as maye subdue hym by the swerde:" it deals at some length with the native Irish and the Anglo-Irish leaders, and says

"The names of the Countyes subjett unto the Kinge's lawes Halff the countye of Uryell (Louth) by estimation

      „   „   Meath

      „   „   Dublyn

      „   „   Kyldare

      „   „   Wexford.

"All the comyn peoplle of the said halff countyes, that obeyeth the Kynge's lawes, for the more parte ben of Iryshe byrthe, of Iryshe habyte and of Iryshe langage[2]." The report continues that tribute was paid by the English settlement to the wild Iryshe:—

"The countye of Uryell payeth yerely to the great Oneyll   40£

      „   „   Meath   „   „   to Ochonour   300£

      „   „   Kyldare „   „   to the said Ochonour 20£

---

[1] *State of Ireland and a Plan for its Reformation*, State Papers, Henry VIII. Vol. II. part iii. pp. 1—30. This report is founded mainly on the ' *Salus Populi* ' of Pandarus. Compare also statements in the same volume of the State Papers, pp. 338—481 as to the scarcity of English.

[2] State Papers, Henry VIII. Vol. II. pt. iii. p. 8.

The Kynge's exchequer payeth yerely to McMurho   80 markes

„ Countye of Wexfor   „   „   „   „ &to Arte Oboy 40£[1]."

And it is plain how greatly the means of exaction of both
the Irish and the English landed systems were pressed upon
the inhabitants of the Pale, for the report says that:—

" What with the extortion of coyne and lyverye dayly, and
wyth the wrongful exactions of osteing money, and of caryage
and cartage dayly, and what with the Kinge's greate subsydye
yerely, and with the said trybute and blak rent to the Kynge's
Iryshe enymyes, and other infynyt extortions and dayly
exactions[2]," they were even more heavily oppressed than the
inhabitants of the Marches.

Henry endeavoured to change this state of affairs by the
enforcement of English rule, and was to a certain limited
extent successful[3]. His assumption of the title of King of Ireland was well received; and by bribing the leading native chiefs
with the spoils of the Church, in the shape of lands formerly
belonging to the Irish abbeys[4], he induced some of them to
surrender their lands and receive them again as feudal tenants.
It would seem, however, that the Irish Princes reserved to
themselves all their former privileges[5]. Mr Froude observes
" Henry did not insist that the Irish, ill-trained as they had
been, should submit at once to English law.... He disavowed
all intentions of depriving the chiefs of their lands, or of con-
fiscating their rights for the benefit of Englishmen. He
desired to persuade them to exchange their system of election
for a feudal tenure, to acknowledge by a formal act of surrender that they held their lordships under the crown...in
return they might retain and administer the more tolerable
of their own Brehon laws, till a more settled life brought with
it a desire for the English common law[6]." By similar gifts
of Church lands Henry won over many of the degenerate

[1] State Papers, Henry VIII. Vol. II.
pt. iii. p. 9.

[2] Ib. pp. 9, 10.

[3] O'Connor Morris, L. Q. Review,
1887, p. 138.

[4] Some of the land in Ireland held

by small crown rents is derived from
these grants.

[5] See Spenser's *View of the State of
Ireland*, 1633, p. 4.

[6] *The English in Ireland*, Froude,
Vol. I. pp. 37, 38.

barons[1], and he also endeavoured to prevent absenteeism, and thus to strengthen the loyal element within the Pale.

This policy, if carried out to the full, might at least have largely increased the English power in Ireland, even if it had not ultimately led to the subjection of the whole island[2]; but the narrow aims of the colonists of the Pale, whose desires appear to have been centred in universal spoliation, and who aimed at nothing but the division of the lands of 'the enemy' between themselves, opposed a barrier to the more liberal methods of the English king. Before long also the religious animosities[3] arising out of the reformation added fuel to the raging furnace of national passions, and brought all the powers of bigotry and intolerance into play in the death struggle of Irish independence.

At first the efforts of Henry to introduce the reformation into Ireland did not raise as much opposition as might have been expected from the Irish lords[4], though the resistance of the clergy[5] rendered the attempt futile. The wars of Elizabeth were in reality inspired by the lust of conquest and the antagonism of race rather than by religious fervour; but from the time when the Stuarts ascended the English throne the crusade of religion began in earnest; and Cromwell and his fanatical soldiery gained those substantial temporal possessions in Ireland (which for the first time justify its being termed a completely conquered country) under the banner of religious bigotry, and in the cause of religious intolerance.

[1] *Land holding in various countries,* Field, p. 250.

[2] O'Connor Morris, *L. Q. R.* p. 138.

[3] " The patriotism of the Irish had taken a peculiar direction. The object of their animosity was not Rome but England; and they had especial reason to abhor those English sovereigns who had been the head of the great schism, Henry the Eighth and Elizabeth. During the vain struggle which two generations of Milesian princes maintained against the Tudors, religious enthusiasm and national enthusiasm became inseparably blended in the minds of the vanquished race. The new feud of Protestant and Papist inflamed the old feud of Saxon and Celt." Lord Macaulay's *Hist. of England,* Vol. I. p. 34.

[4] But the Geraldines were a conspicuous exception.

[5] Cromer, Archbishop of Armagh and Primate of Ireland, was a vigorous opponent of Henry. This is the same Cromer who in 1553 obtained a formal pardon for having made use of the Brehon laws. (Pat. and Close Rolls of Chancery in Ireland, 24 and 25 Hen. VIII.)

The earlier portion of the reign of Elizabeth was marked
by the theoretical confiscation of Ulster, which, however, remained practically unsubdued; by an attempt to levy assess-
ments by Royal authority independent of the sanction of
Parliament; and finally by some claims to lands in Cork under
alleged charters dating from the time of the old Norman
feudal grants[1]. Plans for colonization also were laid before
the English government by those who had no title, but offered
to defray the costs of conquest in consideration of grants from
the conquered territory[2].

The Anglo-Irish lords and Irish chieftains, with no small
reason, felt that the seal of doom was upon them, and the
brewing trouble took form in the rising at first headed by
Sir John Desmond, the treacherous murderer of Henry Davels,
and afterwards by the Earl of Desmond. Religious motives
strengthened this outbreak, and indeed almost created it; but
although aided by a small expedition of Italian and Spanish
volunteers, the futile effort ended in desolation and despair, and
so complete was the ravage and wreck in Munster that "the
lowing of a cow or the sound of a ploughboy's whistle was not
to be heard from Valentia to the rock of Cashel[3]." From the
widespread confiscations which followed, a supply of lands was
obtained, sufficient, it would seem, to have been a most potent
bribe to the new settler class that it was the policy of the English
crown to plant on the Irish soil. Half a million acres[4] escheated
to the crown, and were divided into lots of 12,000, 8,000,
6,000 and 4,000 acres respectively. The rents reserved were
practically nil, an estate at fee farm of 12,000 acres being only
rented at £33. 6s. 8d. for three years, and then at £66. 13s. 4d.
The scheme designed for the plantation was briefly that every

---

[1] Field, pp. 250 and 251.

[2] This method of raising money from
'Undertakers' afterwards became common.

[3] "Whosoever did travel from one
end to the other of all Munster, even
from Waterford to Limerick which is
about six score miles, he should not
meet any man, woman, or child, saving
in towns and cities; nor yet see any
beasts but the very wolves, the foxes,
and other ravening beasts." Quoted by
Hallam, *Const. Hist. of Eng.* vol. III.
pp. 366, 367. And see John Hooker's
dedicatory epistle to Girald. Cambr. in
Holinshed's *Chronicles*, vol. I.

[4] 574,628 acres.

seigniory should be inhabited within seven years on the following system :—" every undertaker of 12,000 acres was bound to plant eighty-six families: his own family was to have 1,600 acres, one chief farmer 400, two good farmers 600, two other farmers 400, fourteen freeholders (each 300) 4,200, forty copyholders (each 100) 4,000, twenty-six cottagers and labourers 800. Other undertakers being bound proportionately[1]."

In 1586 an immense quantity of fertile land was practically going begging; lands were offered at twopence an acre with no rent to be required for the first three years[2], yet the fruitful soil scarce found an owner. By the original design of the plantation the grants of land were to have been conditional on the settlement on the soil by the undertakers of English tenants, but the idea had to be abandoned. The practical failure of the plantation, at any rate, to answer the purpose for which it was designed, i.e. the ousting of the native population, was mainly due to (1) the extensive grants made to particular individuals[3] who themselves remained absentees, making but small and unsuccessful efforts to plant English sub-tenants, and who moreover were not averse to an Irish tenantry (since they paid higher rent than any for which English small holders[4] could be induced to settle); and (2) the short terms for which lands were granted by the English undertakers. The uncertainty of possession and the exactions levied on the tenants prevented any real improvement of the land, and led to its being wastefully impoverished. No buildings worthy of the name were erected, and the wretched slave of the soil lived a life but one degree above that of the animals he tended. Any gathering of wealth brought ruin; coshered by some wandering ex-chief, or rack-rented by some English undertaker, the small holder presented an emblem of misery.

When dealing with the reorganization of much of the Irish land system which took place during the reign of Elizabeth, the

[1] Sigerson, p. 33.
[2] Field, 251.
[3] Sir Walter Raleigh obtained 42,000 acres in Cork and Waterford.
[4] See a passage from Robert Paine's *Briefe Description of Ireland* (1589), quoted p. 35 Sigerson.

'Composition of Connaught,' planned under a Commission issued in 1585, with the object of inducing the nobles of Connaught to surrender their titles and hold instead by letters patent[1] from the crown, should not be passed over. It was one of the first of a succession of legal devices for the change of Irish tenures into feudal ones. Few chieftains, however, agreed to the change, which would have greatly altered the relations of chiefs and people both *inter se* and towards the land. The principle proposed in the change was that a payment of 10s. for every 120 acres should operate as a discharge from all cess, taxation tallage, charges, bearing of soldiers, &c., and that a rent should be payable for the lands; while the customs of Gavelkind and Tanistry were to be abolished. In several of the indentures[2] also the mean freeholders were placed in direct dependence on the crown, a remarkable fact bearing a strong resemblance to the effect of 'quia emptores,' and establishing something greatly like a peasant proprietary. Though this abortive scheme is not of great importance, for few chieftains surrendered under it (though the surrender was widespread under the commission of James the First), still when the plans of Wentworth with regard to Connaught are remembered, an interest is felt in the nature of the titles so unscrupulously attacked: and in regard to those of the Irishry who had surrendered their estates and received a re-grant, it is hard to find words strong enough to describe the injustice of the pretext on which it was attempted to oust them.

In August 1598 the flame of open revolt again broke out, this time in Ulster under Hugh O'Neil (afterwards Earl of Tyrone), and O'Donnell. With the war-cry of religion added to the stored wealth of national hatred[3], indued with a fury

---

[1] By 12 Eliz. c. 4 (Irish) a power had been given by which any of the Irishry or degenerate English were enabled on surrender to obtain grants of their lands by letter patent from the crown—defects appearing in the letters patent issued under this Act, they were remedied by James I. in 1615 by new surrenders and re-grants.

[2] This enactment is to be found in the indentures for Roscommon, Sligo, Mayo and Leitrim—and Dr Sigerson suggests it may have had a bearing on "the after quietness of the western provinces," p. 31.

[3] The dispossession of the Catholic clergy by Elizabeth and the substitution of what has been well termed ' a

such as is almost without parallel, the strife raged. Philip of Spain, smarting from the defeat of his designs on England and burning with a lust for revenge, sent aid, and O'Neil was no ordinary leader; but the doom of destruction was on the Celts. Ravage and ruin was spread broadcast through the land, but the result of the struggle was never really in doubt. No sooner was the conduct of the war entrusted to Mountjoy than the fate of the Irish was sealed, and in 1602 all was over. From the horrors of the prolonged war, as from so many another blood-stained page of Irish history, one can but turn with loathing.

The revolt is important in its ultimate bearing on the history of the Irish land, though no important forfeitures were immediately exacted. The leaders of the rising were treated with singular mercy as one by one they surrendered, O'Neil himself being left in his Earldom; but O'Neil and O'Donnell were marked men. Elizabeth again tried the policy, so often unsuccessful, of a leniency which was neither respected nor understood. Four years later, in the reign of James the First, O'Neil and the Earl of Tyrconnel[1], detected in planning another outbreak, fled the country, and their immense estates escheated to the crown.

Some two millions of acres—the counties of Donegal, Derry, Cavan, Fermanagh, Armagh and Tyrone—were thus placed at the disposal of the English; but, only 511,465 were actually taken up by the crown. The way in which this half million of acres was primarily granted is shown by the following table[2]:

To the Londoners and other undertakers :	209,800
The Bishops' mensal lands	3,413
„ „ termons and erenachs	72,280
„ College of Dublin	9,600

college of shepherds without sheep' let loose upon the people a body of ecclesiastics, who, themselves smarting under their injuries, helped to stir that spirit of rebellion which was simmering throughout the country; but as is remarked by Hallam (vol. III. p. 365) the chances of insurrection would have been tried by the Desmonds and Tyrones, independent of this motive.

[1] Brother of the O'Donnell of the revolt, who died in Spain.

[2] Taken from *Short Hist. of Irish People*, A. G. Richey, p. 605.

For free schools	2,700
To Incumbents for glebes	18,000
The old glebes	1,268
To Deans and Prebends	1,473
„ servitors and natives	116,330
„ impropriations and abbey lands	21,552
The old patentees and forts	38,214
To new corporations	8,887
Restored to Maguire	5,980
Restored to several Irish	1,468

The scheme of plantation drawn up in 1609[1] provided for the settlement upon these lands of large numbers of small tenants, and a colony of Scotch and English Protestants, mainly 'labourers, weavers, mechanics, farmers and merchants,' was established on the escheated territory. Frugal and hardworking the new settlers established an era of apparent prosperity, and until 1641 lived side by side with the native race[2] with less open hostility than might have been expected.

[1] Fully treated of in the next Chapter.

[2] To whom the unappropriated territory, some million and a half acres, had been restored.

PART II.

IRELAND THE SLAVE.

CHAPTER V.

The substitution of English Tenures and the Era of Protestant Ascendency.

THERE is every reason to believe that the changes first systematically introduced in the reign of James the First were conceived in a liberal spirit, and honestly designed to benefit an unhappy country groaning under the yoke of heavy oppressions; but the fatal mistake of implanting a comparatively advanced civilization upon a society unfit to receive it converted what was intended as a benefit into a curse. What would have been the effect of a recognition of the Brehon Law, and an application of the machinery of Courts and determinate sanctions to its system is difficult to say, probably it would have forced into unnatural prominence many customs which had only a theoretical existence[1]; but it is hard in the light of later events not to think that this might have been the less of two evils. The history of the final abolition of the Irish code is simple. Two decisions of the Courts in the reign of James the First, whereby the whole land system of the Brehon Law was crumbled into dust, became of great importance, since they followed the conquests of war, and hence affected practically the whole of Ireland. One, by the decision of all the Judges ('per tous les justices') declared void in law the Irish custom of Gavelkind succession, while the other abolished Tanistry.

The judgment in Gavelkind which is fully reported by Sir John Davies is worthy of close examination. The reasons given in it for the decision are:—

[1] Sir H. Maine considered that this has largely been the result of our recognition in India of the Indian customs.

(1) That the frequent partitions and the removals of the
tenants from one portion to another caused great uncertainty
of possession to be felt, and led to no civil habitations
being erected, or enclosures and improvements made (instancing
the case of Ulster, "which seemed to be all one wilderness
before the new plantation made by the English undertakers
there").

(2) That it differed from Kentish Gavelkind[1] in that the
latter:—

i. Only parted the lands between the next heirs male,
who took estates of inheritance.

ii. Excluded bastards.

iii. Endowed the wife with a moiety.

iv. Permitted females to take in default of males;
none of which characteristics were present in Irish Gavelkind.

(3) That in several ways it resembled the custom of
Gavelkind used in North Wales, which was abolished by
34 Hen. VIII. c. 28.

The judgment therefore says that "for these reasons and
because all the said Irish countries, and the inhabitants of
them, from henceforward, were to be governed by the rules
of the Common Law of England, it was resolved and declared
by all the Judges, that the said Irish custom of Gavelkind was
void in law, not only for the inconvenience and unreasonable-
ness of it, but because it was a mere personal custom and could
not alter the descent of inheritance. And therefore all the
lands in these Irish countries were now adjudged to descend
according to the course of the Common Law, and that wives
should be endowed, and the daughters should be inheritable
to these lands notwithstanding this Irish usage or custom[2]."
This judgment was, by the special order of the lord deputy,
registered amongst the Acts of Council[3].

[1] Of which in reality, however, it
was but a more primitive form. For a
contemporary account of Kentish Gavelkind see *A Treatise of Gavelkind*,
by William Sumner, London, 1660.

[2] Hill, 3, Jacobi. Davies' Reports,
pp. 134—138.

[3] And this provision was added "if
any of the mere Irish had possessed
and enjoyed any portion of land by
this Irish custom of Gavelkind before
the reign of James the First, they
should be continued and established
in it, but that all such should hence-

Not less important than this decision is the one by which the custom of Tanistry was declared void. It was given upon a special verdict found in ejectment between Murrough Mac Bryan, plaintiff, and Cahir O'Callaghan, defendant; the question being whether the title of the heir at Common Law, which lay in the defendant, or the title of the Tanaist, which was the estate of the plaintiff, should prevail. The case remained in the King's Bench for three or four years, and was argued several times, while the Judges on different occasions delivered their opinions on the various points raised. The suit terminated in an agreement by consent for a division; it was, however, finally settled by the Court that "the said custom of Tanistry was void in itself, and abolished when the Common Law of England was established."

By these two decisions the law of a nation, which, whatever its faults, was ingrained in their national life, and regarded by them with that unreasoning devotion which is one of the curious contradictions of the Celtic nature, was swept away. While giving all due credit to the disinterested motives of the English Crown and its advisers, and to the strict impartiality of the judicial decisions, there seems to be no doubt from the lesson of history that a grave error was committed and a substantial injustice done. Despite the recognition by the Brehon Laws of the existence of individual property, a large majority of the land seems to have been ruled by a more or less modified form of the customs of Tanistry and Gavelkind; and though the extensive growth of the power of the chief makes it evident that in reality the practical development of tenure, and even of primogeniture, was not far distant, still the native Irish were as far from recognizing the fact as were the English rulers who implanted the feudal system upon them. The ignorant Irish tribesman had no notion that the exactions of his chieftain were by imperceptible degrees taking the form of rent, on the contrary he was driven by them to cling more closely to the soil by a hundred ties of attachment; while the chief more

forth be adjudged and descend according to the Common Law." See also Furlong's *Landlord and Tenant;* and   Plowden's *Historical Review of the state of Ireland.*

and more regarded the land as a mere source of revenue. Into the hands of the law officials of James the First was intrusted the impossible task of solving satisfactorily a land problem in which each free member of a tribe who received land in fee would think that he got no more than his due, while those who were neglected, or whose portions not being to their taste must have longed for the old system of redistribution, would imagine themselves forcibly robbed. To these we must also add a certain class of tribesmen, owners of small portions of the tribe-land, who were altogether disregarded by Sir John Davies. The Attorney-General in his letter to the Earl of Salisbury in 1607 when describing the manner in which the land was portioned amongst the septs, and pointing out that almost every acre had a several owner owing to the expansion of the system of distribution by Gavelkind, says, "we made every enquiry what portion of land or services every man held in every ballibetagh[1], beginning with such first as had lands and services; and after naming such as had the greatest quantity of land and so descending into such as possess only two taths; then we stayed, for lower we could not go, because we knew the purpose of the State was only to establish such freeholders as are fit to serve on juries[2]." It is necessary also to bear in mind the position of the next generation of 'mere Irish' to those to whom the grants were made. Thus A, a free member of the sept, receives a grant of lands in fee—he has issue four sons, B, C, D and E. Under the old system each on his birth would have become a member of the sept, he would have looked on all the lands of the sept as in a sense his property, since from them in due course his allotment would have been received. Under the new system B, the eldest, is alone entitled to lands, and these only on his father's death. Assuredly C, D and E

---

[1] The ancient Irish land measures differ so much that it is hard to explain what extent of land is denoted by any term. According to Sir John Davies, in Fermanagh a ballybetagh is equal to 16 taths, but he then goes on to say that Fermanagh containing 51 ballybetaghs is well nigh as large as Monaghan which contains 100. See fully on this subject Skene's *Celt. Scot.*, Vol. III. pp. 153—170.

[2] Appended to the early editions of the *Discoverie*.

(and probably *B* also) would think that the hated English had robbed them of their birthright. The task of Sir John Davies was truly no light one, and the way in which he viewed the situation and his manner of dealing with it are worthy of the closest attention. Speaking of Tanistry and Gavelkind he says, "these two Irish customs made all their possessions uncertain, being shuffled, and changed, and removed so often from one to another, by new elections and partitions; which uncertainty of estates hath bin the true cause of such desolation and barbarism in this land, as the like hath not been seen in any country that professed the name of Christ[1]." He goes on to state that the Act passed in 12 Eliz.[2], enabling the Lord Deputy to take surrenders and re-grant estates to the Irishry, was defective, since (1) few lords made such surrenders, and (2) "they which made surrenders of entire counties obtained grants of the whole againe to themselves only, and to no other, and all in demesne. In passing of which grants there was no care taken of the inferiour Septes of people, inhabiting and possessing these counties under them, but they held their severall portions in course of Tanistry and Gavelkind, and yielded the same Irish duties or exactions, as they did before[3]." Then alluding to the two Commissions which issued under James the First, the one to accept surrenders and to make re-grants, and the other to strengthen defective titles, he states; "in the execution of which Commissions there hath ever bin had a special care, to settle and secure the Under-Tenants, to the end that there might be a repose and establishment of every subject's estate[4];" the following being the plan adopted; "when an Irish lord doth offer to surrender his country, his surrender is not immediately accepted, but a commission is first awarded to enquire of these special points. First, of the quantity and limits of the land

---

[1] *Discoverie*, p. 170.

[2] The instructions given to the Earl of Suffolk in 1560 by Elizabeth suggested that the Irish chiefs should surrender their estates and take grants in tail male; the Act of 1569 (12 Eliz. c.

[4] Irish) recites that the Irish had petitioned to surrender and authorizes the granting of letters patent.

[3] *Discoverie*, pp. 270, 271.

[4] *Discoverie*, p. 273.

whereof he is the reputed owner. Next how much himself doth hold in demesne, and how much is possessed by his tenants and followers. And thirdly, what customs, duties and services he doth yearly receive out of those lands. This inquisition being made and returned, the lands which are found to bee the lord's proper possessions in demesne, are drawn into a *Particular*; and his Irish duties; as *cosherings, cessings, Rents of Butter and Oatmeale* and the like; are reasonably valued and reduced into certaine *summes of Money* to be paide yearely in lieu thereof. This being done, the surrender is accepted; and thereupon a grant passed, not of the whole country, as was used in former times, but of those lands only, which are found in the lord's possession, and of those certaine summes of money, as rents issuing out of the rest. But the lands which are found to be possessed by the tenants, are left unto them, respectively charged with these certain rents only, in lieu of all uncertain Irish exactions. In like manner upon all *Grants* which have passed by virtue of the Commission, for defective titles, the Commissioners have taken special caution, for the preservation of the estates of all particular tenants."

Sir John Davies had, it is evident, clearly grasped the fact of the proprietary rights of the members of the tribe in the tribe-land; but the sweeping nature of the change introduced, and the conflicting character of the rights involved, rendered his settlement an unstable one. Even if the inferior members of the sept were, as stated by him, satisfied and encouraged by the settlement and security of their tenure, the chief was grievously wounded by the restriction of what he considered his inalienable rights[1]; and subsequent events almost obliterated the class of freehold owners which Sir John Davies had laboured to create. The mode, however, in which the Irish tribesmen were considered in relation to the land is plain, and the system adopted amounts to an acknowledgment of the claims of the tribal freeman to an estate in the land. The injury inflicted upon the Irish peasantry lay indeed not so much in the

[1] See "The Historical Claims of Tenant-Right," *Nineteenth Century,*   January, 1881, p. 27, Seebohm.

introduction of the English tenures, as in the after refusal to
recognize the rights of the tenantry established under the
compulsory reorganizations of the land system. In the Commission for making shires in 1605 the principle of the existence of tenant-right was also recognized: for the conduct
of many persons who, pretending to be lords, had expelled
ancient tenants or imposed exactions upon them "under pretence that the said tenantes or freeholders are but tenantes-
at-will, albeit they and their ancestors have enjoyed the same
by course of descent for many hundred yeares past," is repro-
bated[1].

In 1608, on the flight abroad of the two Earls[2], their estates
were, as has been described in the last chapter, forfeited to the
Crown. It will be necessary to go at some length into the
nature and regulations of the colony which was planted on the
most fertile portion of this territory, and it will be seen that
at first sight the plan devised was not inequitable. Still it
must be remembered that in many ways this plantation
was a deliberate undoing of the work of Sir John Davies.
The rights of the newly created freeholders obtained little
recognition, and were frequently infringed on behalf of the
settlers, and even where their rights were not actually disturbed a feeling of insecurity was given to the new tenures,
the one thing it was most important to avoid. It is perhaps
worthy of note that it has been alleged that the disgavelling
which preceded the forfeitures was part of a deep plot of the
English, who considered, on the analogy of the Gavelkind lands
in Kent, that Irish Gavelkind lands would be more protected
against escheat than those held by knight-service. The faults
of the suggestion are obvious. It is true that the very nature
of the Brehon Law is far too archaic to recognize such forms
of ownership as the principle of escheat involves, but the
theory of Gavelkind had never before been allowed to interfere
with the rights of the Crown in Ireland to escheats, and both
Earls held from the Crown long before the 'Case of Gavelkind.' The suggestion is a very fair example of the amount of

---

[1] Sigerson, *Hist. of Land Tenure*   [2] See ante, p. 63.
and Land Classes, p. 104 (note.)

ingenious perversion which is always applied to the acts of the English in Ireland.

The plantation of the colony in Ulster was evidently elaborated with no small care by James the First and his advisers[1], who adopted in the main a project drawn up by the Privy Council of Ireland[2]. Orders and Conditions[3] were issued for the guidance of the undertakers who applied for grants of land, commencing as follows:—" His Majesty in his princely bounty, not respecting his own profit, but the public peace and welfare of the kingdom, is graciously pleased to distribute the said lands to such of his subjects, as well of Great Britain as of Ireland, as being of merit and ability shall seek the same with a mind not only to benefit themselves, but to do service to the Crown and common wealth." The most noticeable points of the proposed scheme of plantation were that the lands to be distributed were divided into lots of 1,000, 1,500 and 2,000 English acres respectively, and the undertakers to whom such lots were committed were separated into three classes, namely:

(1) " English or Scottish, as well servitors[4] as others, who are to plant their portions with English, or inland Scottish inhabitants."

(2) " Servitors in the kingdom of Ireland, who may take mere Irish, English or inland Scottish tenants at their choice."

(3) " Natives of Ireland who are to be made freeholders[5]."

The rents of the English and Scottish undertakers were fixed at £5. 6s. 0d. for every 1,000 acres, and no charge of rent was to be made for the first two years. The nature of their tenure was as follows. Every grantee of 2,000 acres was to hold by knight's service in capite ; and every grantee of 1,000 acres was to hold in common socage, no wardships being exacted upon the first descent of that land. The undertakers and their tenants were to erect within two years castles and

---

[1] Though the plantation was projected by the king and by Bacon it was chiefly carried into effect by Sir Arthur Chichester, who appears to have displayed great resources, and who received a large allotment himself.

[2] See Harris' *Hibernica*, where this project is quoted in full, pp. 105—120.

[3] See Harris' *Hibernica*, p. 123 et seq.

[4] The servitors were of two kinds, (1) great officers of the state, (2) rich adventurers from England.

[5] Harris' *Hibernica*, p. 114.

buildings; they were forbidden to alienate their holdings to the 'mere Irish,' and were not allowed to create tenancies at will. The undertakers were bound within two years to place upon their lands a competent number of tenants and the rent was to be a fixed sum; special proviso being made against cuttings, cosherings, and other Irish exactions[1]. The above rules appear to be framed in a liberal and thoughtful spirit, and show much consideration for the best interests of the land. The rules applicable to the Irish natives who were admitted as freeholders also seem to be both magnanimous and well considered. They are mainly as follows:— their estates to be in fee farm, the yearly rent being £10. 13s. 4d. for each portion of 1,000 acres, and no rent to be payable for the first year; their tenures to be similar to those of the other undertakers with a proviso of forfeiture on rebellion. They were to inhabit their lands and to build castles and houses; but no Irish exactions were to be taken[2]. As regards the class of native small-holders in Ulster, it would seem that these rules might have afforded a satisfactory position, but unfortunately the plantation was not ultimately carried out quite as designed. The native Irish were frequently unjustly ousted to make way for new English settlers, and the engine of English law, the theory and methods of which were completely strange to the native race, was only too often used to establish claims of the Crown in the native holdings. In other parts of Ireland this was even more the case than in Ulster, "in King's and Queen's Counties, and in those of Leitrim, Longford and Westmeath, 385,000 acres were adjudged to the Crown, and 66,000 in that of Wicklow," so that, though much was re-granted to the Irish, it shook their sense of possession[3]; while the flagrant injustice with which the claims of the Crown were often prosecuted, rankled in their minds. Meanwhile the energetic class of artizans and me-

[1] See Orders and Conditions for the planters of Ulster given in Harris' *Hibernica*, from a copy printed in 1608.

[2] Harris' *Hibernica*, p. 129. The lands which had been lost to the Church during the late troubles were restored, while the beneficed clergy were cared for by more provision being made for them. And see ante, pp. 63, 64.

[3] Hallam's *Constitutional History*, Vol. III. ch. 18, p. 377.

chanics of the English settlement throve and prospered a-
mazingly, and the sun of prosperity seemed at last breaking
through the heavy pall of misgovernment and misery which
had enveloped Ireland's history. The forfeitures from which
the grants had been derived, however, had cast without support upon the land a body of improvident, vicious and dangerous men, the descendants of the former chiefs; and the
weapon of religious strife lay ready to their hands. As early
as 1611 there were not wanting signs of brewing trouble to be
detected by the far-seeing[1].

On the surface all went well. The Act 13 Jac. I. c. 5[2], re-
peals many of the statutes in which the Irish are treated as
the common enemy, and extends to all the king's subjects the
same laws; while the language of the statute reads in striking
contrast to that of earlier legislation—"Whereas in former
times...the natives of this realm of Irish blood...were for the
most part in continual hostility with the English, and with
those who did descend of the English, and therefore the said
Irish were held and accounted and in divers statutes and
records were termed and called Irish enemies. Forasmuch as
the cause of the said difference and of the making of the said
laws and statutes doth now cease, in that all the natives and
inhabitants of this kingdom, without difference or distinction
are taken into his majesty's protection, and do now live under
one law, by means whereof a perfect agreement is or ought to
be settled betwixt all of his majesty's subjects in this realm.
And forasmuch as there is no better means to settle peace and
tranquillity in this kingdom, being now inhabited with many
worthy persons born in his majesty's several kingdoms, than
by abolishing the said laws and giving them free liberty to
commerce and match together, so that they may grow into one
nation, and there be so utter oblivion and extinguishment of
all former differences and discords between them; be it enacted
...that all the said laws be for ever utterly repealed[3]."

The Ulster settlement in the course of years accumulated
certain customary modes of dealing with the tenant's interest in

---

[1] See the report of Sir George Carew.   [3] See Froude, *Eng. in Ireland*, p. 70.
[2] (Irish).

the land.   At the present time these exist in the much discuss-
ed "Ulster custom[1]."   Its origin is uncertain, but it has plainly
been built up partially on rude notions of equity, and partially
on a blending of the Irish notions with those of the settlers.
The customs as to land tenure of the Scotch and Welsh tenants
planted in Ulster must have been in many ways similar to
those of their Irish neighbours, and it is possible that the Irish
notions were gradually assimilated to a theory of land tenancy
strongly resembling copyhold.   Unfortunately the Calvinistic
Protestantism of the settlement did something towards adding
to the discordant nature of the social system and the animosity
of the dispossessed owners of the soil.   The Catholics daily
gained strength by union in misfortune, and became more
and more impatient of the existence of the alien plantation.
No excuse, however, for the terrible flood of butchery, cruelty
and massacre which the inhuman insurrection of 1641 produced
is possible.   To the end of time there will rest on the shield of
Ireland's honour the bloodstain of this debauch of ruthless
slaughter.   The real cause of the outbreak is rather to be
found in the land troubles[2] than in religious differences.   The
scheme of a plantation in Connaught had been advancing with
gigantic strides[3].   The Commission on defective titles had
extended its fatal grasp all over the country; nor did the
patents granted under James the First's Commission prove
much protection[4], despite that large sums had often been paid
as composition to remedy defects.   The despicable discoverers
laboured hard, and titles were infamously impeached.   Four-
fifths of Connaught were proved in strict construction to belong
to the Crown[5], and the methods of Wentworth, now Earl of
Strafford, produced a frenzy of rage, the aid not merely of

[1] See post, pp. 117—123.
[2] Among the complaints of the leaders of the Rebellion is found a protest
against "The avoidance of grants of
lands and liberties by quirks and quid-
dities of the law," Sigerson, p. 74.
[3] A plan of plunder more disgraceful
(founded as it was upon the omission

of the mere legal formality of the en-
rolment of grants made in the time of
Elizabeth and James I.) it is hard to
conceive.
[4] *The Cromwellian Settlement*, Prendergast, p. 47.
[5] *The Eng. in Ireland*, Froude, p. 80.

chicane but even of torture[1] being called in to assist the general spoliation. The Connaught Commission paid no heed to the agreement which in 1634 had been made with Charles the First that only sixty years' title need be shown[2]. Deeds and papers had perished in the many wars of those disturbed times, and the Celt, loving the land as only a Celt can, saw it about to be torn from him wholesale. On the 23rd of October, 1641, the massacre commenced, and the lowest estimate of those who perished is 37,000, while Mr Froude believes that before the insurrection was suppressed more than half a million[3] had succumbed.

However varied the causes which led to the insurrection, to the England of the Puritans it bore but one aspect, and Cromwell when he landed in 1649 came as the champion of the Protestant cause, to revenge with fire and sword the evil deeds of the 'Popish fiends.' How complete his conquest was is a matter of history, and a grim picture is drawn by the statement that so was the country wasted that even the victorious English army well nigh starved. The bearing of Cromwell's conquest, and the subsequent confiscation of more than a third of the land of Ireland, on the history of the land law was immense. High and low, Irish chieftain and Irish peasant, together with the descendants of many of the English settlers of the various earlier settlements, were proscribed on the ground of their religion, their estates passing into the hands of the Puritan soldiery. The half depopulated country, thousands of the inhabitants of which were shipped to the West Indies or driven to take refuge on the Continent, was colonized by Saxons of Calvinistic faith; yet under the 'iron rule' there was prosperity, buildings and plantations were made, and the value and rent of land increased daily. The principle of the Cromwellian Settlement was the foundation of a Protestant military colony, extending over all the most fruitful portion of the land. The native Irish were to be banished to Connaught, which

[1] O'Connor Morris, *L. Q. Review*, 1887, p. 139. And see the case of the Byrnes of Wicklow. Carte's *Life of Ormonde*, bk. 1, p. 74.

[2] See Field, p. 253 (note).

[3] Following Sir William Petty, see Froude, *Eng. in Ireland*, Vol. I. p. 125.

Cromwell determined to make a second Wales, only two classes of persons being exempted from transplantation, (1) those who could prove 'constant good affection,' and (2) the mere earth-tillers, viz. 'all husbandmen, plowmen, labourers, artificers and others of the inferior sort.' The settlement, however, when established differed in many ways from the military landlordism which had been intended. Land bonds had been issued to the adventurers in 1642, and money had been advanced on the security of nearly a million acres. Again in 1653, in order to meet the arrears of pay due to Cromwell's army and sums still due to the adventurers, a most thorough act of confiscation had been passed. The debenture bonds payable in land which had been issued to defray military expenses passed into various hands; and the similar bonds issued to Cromwell's own soldiers[1] had in many cases been disposed of by them; still the country largely passed into the hands of the men who had conquered it. A study of Dr Petty's[2] *History of the Down Survey*[3] conveys a clear notion of the great practical difficulties of the working out in detail, within reasonable time and with any approach to justice, of the allotments of forfeited land. "It is difficult to imagine a work more full of perplexity and uncertainty than to locate 32,000 officers, soldiers and followers, with adventurers, settlers and creditors of every kind and class, having different and uncertain claims on lands of different and uncertain value in detached parcels scattered over two-thirds of the surface of Ireland[4]."

The two races of English and Irish had long been gradually taking the respective positions of landlord and tenant. The forfeitures at this time spread this relation over nine-tenths

---

[1] The form of these debenture bonds is illustrated by a facsimile given in Mr Prendergast's *Cromwellian Settlement*, which runs as follows:

"Upon composition and agreement made with...for...arrears for service in Ireland from.... There remains due from the Commonwealth to the said... executors, administrators or assigns the sum of...which is to be satisfied to the said...executors, administrators or as-

signs out of the rebels' houses, tenements and hereditaments in Ireland or other land, houses, tenements and hereditaments there in the dispose of the Commonwealth of England. Signed and sealed at Dublin the—day of—1658."

[2] Afterwards Sir William Petty.

[3] 1655—6. Published in 1851 by the Dublin Archæological Society.

[4] Notes to *History of Survey*, p. 338.

of the country[1]. The most important point in the Cromwellian Settlement having regard to its future bearing on the land question is the position of those Irish peasantry who were not transplanted with the swordsmen into Connaught. The earth-tillers were kept in their holdings for several reasons; firstly, they had always been a fairly quiet and toilsome class, and when freed from the influence of the disquieting element of the transplanted fighting men might be expected to develop into a peaceful tenantry; secondly, there was no sufficient supply of English to take the lowest positions in the social scale. It has been seen that under the change of tenures effected by Sir John Davies a large proportion of the native Irish became freehold owners. By the confiscations following Cromwell's conquest nearly all trace of the Irish owners was swept away, and the position in law of the tenants was completely altered. No longer considered freeholders subject to a quit rent, they were in future treated merely as " commercial tenants under contract or if without contracts as mere tenants at will[2]." There is, however, a very important fact to be considered, namely, that there is no doubt, despite the apparently precarious nature of the tenant's position, that he was at that time considered to have a vested interest in the land. There exists indeed a formal recognition of some degree of tenant-right, for Sir W. Petty when officially surveying the country in the interests of the new owners excepted from his gross valuation of the confiscated lands the value of the tenant's interest in their holdings[3], stating that the benefit of leases and the value of the tenant's improvements upon the said land is one-third—£216,000[4]. This appears to prove conclusively that he did not consider them mere tenants at will.

When Charles the Second was restored, and sober England lapsed for one solitary portion of her history into high carnival,

[1] O'Connor Morris, L. Q. Review, 1887, p. 141.

[2] Seebohm, "The Historical Claims of Tenant-Right," Nineteenth Century, 1881.

[3] Seebohm, "The Hist. Claims of Tenant-Right," and Sir W. Petty's Political Anatomy of Ireland. Also The History of the Down Survey, 1655—6, published in 1851 by the Dublin Archæological Society.

[4] This valuation included the value of their cabins.

the hearts of the conquered party in Ireland were beating high
with hope. Royalists who had ventured and lost all, clamoured
for a guerdon from Irish lands; the transplanted landholders
saw themselves again in fancy installed in their homes; and the
holders under the Cromwellian Settlement trembled for their
possessions. The final arrangement came as a terrible blow
to many. There were difficulties of no small degree in the
way of the advisers of Charles, for his father had ratified the
Act under which money, on the security of Irish land, was
advanced by the adventurers in 1642, and this the king was
therefore bound to support. In 1660 the Commission appointed
to consider the Irish claims commenced its sittings. It was
decided that those who were able to prove themselves innocent
of complicity with the original outbreak were to be reinstated
in their lands, those in possession being compensated by other
grants—the lands still unallotted under the Act of 1653 and
the new forfeitures from the old opponents of Charles the First
being available for this purpose. The Act of Settlement
14 & 15 Car. II. c. 2, carried out this policy, and a Court of
Claims tried the cases in detail[1]. To a very large extent the
Cromwellian settlers managed to retain possession of their
lands, yet more settlers were ousted than there was land elsewhere to satisfy, and a second Act became necessary. This Act,
17 & 18 Car. II. c. 2 (1665), compelled the soldiers, adventurers,
and debenture holders to be content with two-thirds of the
land they had been entitled to under the Cromwellian settlement, and barred all hope of restitution to the 3,000 Irish who
had not yet been adjudged innocent. In the vast majority of
cases these latter had certainly been guilty, but they were
naturally enraged at the loss of their possessions without a trial.
The result of the Commission may be stated to be that while
before the rebellion the Irish Catholics held some two-thirds of
the kingdom, more than half of these possessions were now lost[2].

---

[1] It seems that nearly 7,800,000 acres
came before the Court of Claims.—Sigerson, p. 96. See *Letters of the Earl
of Essex* as to the competition for
lands.

[2] Hallam, Vol. III. chap. 18, p. 33.
A considerable portion of land in Ireland is held by small quit rents under
letters patent which date from the Acts
of Settlement and Explanation.

In reviewing the history of landed relations in Ireland up to the reign of Charles the Second it must be remembered that if heavy burdens had been exacted from the inferior class of holders, the higher class were themselves the victims of no ordinary oppression. The onerous nature of the incidents of the feudal system pressed most heavily on the whole of the Irish colony; repeatedly the complaint is made that heavy as were the exactions levied by the irregular charges of coygne and livery, they were less grievous than the exactions of the king's officers. It is perhaps no wonder that the lords were little less averse than their tenants to practically free themselves from the feudal bond. The overthrow of the feudal incidents[1], and the substitution of socage tenures for knight service, which the necessities of his situation enabled the lords to exact from Charles the Second, was undoubtedly the downfall of a system of flagrant evil. Had the improved position of the landlord class led to their extending a merciful forbearance to the peasant earth-tillers, half the accumulated wrongs of the history of the Irish land law might never have arisen. The prevalent custom, however, of looking to Irish land as a source of revenue merely, divorced from all reciprocal duties of just management—which led to the creation of the pestilent class of middlemen, and to a system under which the lands of an absentee owner[2] were let six deep—prevented any amelioration of the position of the peasant occupier.

With the accession of James the Second rose the cause of the Catholic party in Ireland. James was fully aware that the Irish troubles sprang more from the distinctions of race than from differences of creed[3], and had his proceedings been marked by a determination quietly to enforce the existing state of affairs, rather than by efforts in the interests of one class to overthrow a settlement sanctioned by twenty-five years' possession under the solemn guarantee of Parliament, much

[1] The Court of Wards and Liveries was in effect discontinued after 1645, and formally abolished by 12 Charles II. c. 24, and 14 & 15 Car. II. sess. 4, c. 19 (Irish).

[2] "Three-fourths of the land at one time, always more than half, belonged to the absentees." Field, p. 263.

[3] See Lord Macaulay's *Hist. of England*, Vol. I. p. 393.

bloodshed might have been avoided.   Had he at the same time
striven to ameliorate the position of the native small holders
by extending to them some measure ot certainty of tenure;
and while extinguishing the extravagant hopes of resumption
cherished by the old proprietors of large domains endeavoured
to reconcile them with the existing settlement, it is possible that
no great difficulties might ever again have arisen; for the condition of the colony was now comparatively prosperous, as was
clearly shown by the fact that rents had almost doubled[1].   His
action, however, was widely different.   Tyrconnell laboured to
undo the work of the Acts of Settlement, and to extirpate the
Protestant interest.   At the time when William landed in
England, in the Court of the Exchequer at Dublin crowded
with Irish applicants armed with writs of ejectment and tres-
pass, no Protestant title, however established, seemed safe.
Finally in 1688 the Catholic party, under the cloak of the cause
of the exiled James, again took arms.   James landed in 1689,
and the Irish and Catholics regarded him as the one who was to
restore to them their inheritance.   A Parliament met at Dublin;
the Acts of Settlement were repealed; and the old owners, who
had been ousted from land which was barren of all save the
good gifts of nature, were replaced on land which the industry,
the labour and the capital of others had made fruitful exceedingly.
Attainders overwhelmed the Protestant owners; but the cause
of James was but a house of cards.   After the battle of the
Boyne the revival of the Protestant supremacy was but a
matter of time, and in 1691 the Treaty of Limerick was signed,
which proved but a feeble protection to the native race.   Again
the tide of change rolled over the Irish lands, and the Commissioners appointed for the purpose of restoring the property
of the Protestants entered on their difficult task; but so complicated were the rights involved that the Settlement took
some years.   The large confiscations of the estates of king
James and his adherents offered new sources for grants[2], which

---

[1] See Lord Macaulay's *Hist. of England*, Vol. I. p. 393.

[2] The forfeitures of land belonging
to the adherents of James II. are

given by Wakefield as amounting to
"1,060,792 acres, which being worth
£211,623 a year at 6 years' purchase
for a life and 13 years for an inherit-

it is to be regretted were often given to those who possessed
no claim to them save Royal favour[1], and who were far from
being the most fitted to deal with the involved problem of
Irish land rights[2].

That the bitterness of many unhealed wounds lay between
the class who ruled and the class who tilled the land, was calculated naturally to produce oppression on the one hand and
hatred on the other. This was increased by the fact that
among the class of earth-tillers, reduced to the lowest step of
the social ladder, were not merely the descendants of the old
tribal freeman, but also the descendants of the noblest houses of
the chieftains; men who to the hatred of nation for nation, and
creed for creed, added the bitterness always felt by the superior
reduced to bondage to one whom he considers immeasurably
his inferior. The sympathies of the subject people were all
against the dominant class. Freebooters, the relics of the army
of James the Second, lived by rapine and exaction; yet says the
Statute of William the Third[3], "the Popish inhabitants chose
rather to suffer strangers to be robbed and despoiled of their
goods than to apprehend the offenders, the greater part of
whom were people of the same country and harboured by the
inhabitants." With a short-sighted policy, moreover, the evil
effects of which were manifold, the English nation kept the
Irish native race enthralled to the soil. The doors which might
have been opened to them by the encouragement of manufacture and trade were kept resolutely closed. Had this been
different, by teaching the Irish to look away from the vexed
subject of the land for their sustenance, the strained relations

ance amounted to £2,685,130. Out of
these lands the estates restored to the
old proprietors under the articles of
Limerick and Galway were valued at
£724,923 and those restored by Royal
favour at £260,863. And after these
deductions and several other allow-
ances, the gross value of the estates
forfeited from the 13th of February,
1688, amounted to £1,699,343." *Account of Ireland.*

[1] By the Resumption Act of 1699

these estates were afterwards reclaimed
and vested in trustees for sale for the
benefit of the English nation.

[2] The Commission of 1699 revealed
a mass of jobbery into which it is impossible to enter here, but the case of
Lady Orkney alone is sufficient to
condemn the whole transaction. See
Froude, *Eng. in Ireland*, Vol. I. pp. 245
—248.

[3] 7 Will. III. c. 21 (Irish), and see
Froude, Vol. I. p. 262.

between the two classes of landholders might have been eased, and the two races drawn together by bonds of mutual interest in commercial dealings. On the contrary, fresh restrictions were ever and anon placed on the development of native industry. The prohibitions and duties imposed on the export and manufacture of wool and woollen goods[1], and then on linen; the restrictions on the importation into England of cattle, and the far-reaching wrong inflicted by the Merchant Navigation Act, 1663[2], aggravated the evils of the land system by increasing the class of those dependent upon the soil. Moreover, the provisions which prohibited Papists from sitting in Parliament[3], and which took away from them the elective franchise, prevented the position of the conquered people being ably advocated, and hindered the bitter cry of their wrongs from adequate utterance. It is, alas, but seldom realized how immense an influence the laws regulating the social relations and commercial dealings of a community have upon the amelioration or aggravation of its land system. Where the problem of a community is presented by the abject condition of its lowest class, and that class is found to cling to the land with an unreasoning tenacity which ends only with life itself, it may be predicted with certainty that there exists, either at that time or in the history of the community, some cause other than mere national aspirations. Land, by the fatal policy of England[4], was made the vital necessity of the Celtic race. Half the land hunger of the Irish peasantry has its root in the transmitted idea that the possession of land is an essential of existence. The legislation which for a century deliberately shut the door to the growth of Irish commerce, and which systematically laboured to reduce to subjection the native race, bound them to the land by barring all other means not only of wealth but of bare subsistence. It will be seen later how this fact

---

[1] 13 & 14 Car. II. c. 18, and 10 & 11 Will. III. c. 10.
[2] See Field, p. 266.
[3] 3 Will. & Mary, c. 2.
[4] Hallam says, when dealing with the Penal and Commercial Codes, "To have exterminated the Catholics by the sword, or expelled them like the Moriscoes of Spain, would have been little more repugnant to justice and humanity, but incomparably more politic."

rendered the pretty paper theory of free contractual relations in
land dealing a source of desperate misery. How was it possible
for such a method to hold for a moment when a commodity of
which the supply was limited was hungered after by a whole
community with a wild desire, caused not only by national
predilections and present necessities, but also by an ingrained
sentiment, graven upon their characters by a mass of legislation
which had driven them to the soil for their very being?

Not only the Commercial Codes but also the illiberal and
inhumane Penal Code tended to aggravation of the land difficulty. Designed as it was to reduce to the lowest grade the
scanty remnant of those Catholics who retained recognizable
proprietary rights in the soil, its result was to increase the class
of those dependent upon the land for their sustenance. A cur-
sory glance at some of these provisions, which constitute such
a blot on the Statute Book, will illustrate this proposition.
Catholics were prohibited from taking a freehold or a mortgage
of lands, and if they succeeded to such must conform within six
months or forfeit[1] to the next Protestant heir. Their lands
were gavelled[2] and descended to the children equally, but subject to the proviso that if the eldest son conformed, the father
merely had an estate for life, the reversion in fee resting with
the son[3]. A Protestant heiress who married a Catholic forfeited her lands to her next of kin, and a Protestant man
marrying a Papist became himself liable to all the disabilities of a Catholic[4]. The whole weight of the law tended to
reduce the Catholic interest in the land to mere tenancies at
will. Leases save for thirty-one years or less, and then at a
rent of two-thirds value, were forbidden them; while should
the profit rent of the land be found to exceed the allowed third
the benefit of the lease was transferred to the Protestant who

---

[1] See O'Connor Morris, p. 143.

[2] It has been well pointed out that
this provision is a strong confirmation
of the good intention with which the
abolition of Irish Gavelkind was carried out by Sir John Davies, for here
it is restored for the express purpose
of destroying the class to whom it was
applied, proving that it was really considered a destructive custom.

[3] What kind of landlord was a son
who abjured his faith for this reason
likely to be?

[4] 9 Will. III. c. 3 (Irish), and see for
further repressive legislation 2 Anne
c. 3 (Irish) and 2 Anne c. 6 (Irish).

made the discovery. This last provision encouraged a most
baneful system of informers, and completely prevented the
proper cultivation of the soil. The enactments of Parliament,
moreover, were imitated in various bye-laws passed by local
corporations, with the result of excluding the Catholics from
every useful branch of trade.

It is not remarkable that, labouring under the monstrous
burden of the Penal and Commercial Codes, the Catholic
owners and the native race generally were reduced to a most
abject condition, and lapsed into mere occupiers, holding practically only tenancies at will. Nor were the native Irish and
the Catholics the only persons who were thus cast on the
land. The descendants of many of the Colonists of the
Cromwellian Settlement became as Irish as the natives, and
were involved with them in the common ruin; while the descendants of many colonists of earlier settlements were reduced
to the same condition in a rather curious manner. The English
undertakers who received estates in the various settlements on
the condition of planting a certain number of English tenants
had frequently treated those colonists, whom they induced by
promises of freehold estates to go to Ireland, with great injustice. The actual lease for life or lives, or grant of an estate
in fee, was refused them, and they were compelled to put up
with mere possession and a parol agreement. This frequently
satisfied them, since when livery of seisin was at its height
possession bore many binding traits[1], and the idea that it
involved determinate rights was long-lived; but by a statute
of William the Third[2] any estate that they might have
deemed themselves the owners of was swept away. This
statute enacted that after 1696 "all leases, estates, interests,
freeholds or terms of years, or any uncertain interest of, into
or out of any messuages, manors, lands, tenements or hereditaments, made and created by livery of seisin only, or by

[1] In Bracton's time the law protected
possession, even if untitled and vicious,
against property; but by the time of
Littleton the power of seisin was greatly diminished. "The Beatitude of
Seisin," F. W. Maitland, *L. Q. Review*,
1888.

[2] 7 Will. 3, sess. 1. c. 12 (Irish) and
see Sigerson, p. 101.

parol and not put in writing and signed by the parties so making and creating the same or their agents, thereunto authorized by writing, shall have the force and effect of leases and estates at will only." Practically this is an extension of the Statute of Frauds[1] to Ireland, and mischievous as that statute has sometimes proved in England, it would in the very nature of things prove more so in Ireland, for an unlearned tenantry would be totally unable to understand such a departure from their parol customs. It has been remarked with much justice that this statute "produced written leases in England, but it only legalized gross general exactions in Ireland."

How complete was the subjection of the native race during the hundred years that followed 1691 it is hard to paint in sufficiently forcible colours: Swift, writing in 1731, said, "The estates of the Papists are very few, crumbling into small parcels, and daily diminishing; their common people are sunk in poverty, ignorance and cowardice, and of as little consequence as women and children. Their nobility and gentry are at least one half ruined, banished or converted. They all soundly feel the smart of what they suffered in the last Irish war. Some of them are already retired into foreign countries: others, as I am told, intend to follow them; and the rest, I believe to a man, who still possess any lands, are absolutely resolved never to hazard them again for the sake of establishing their superstition[2]." As is pointed out by Lord Macaulay, the native race found no champion even among those English who most studiously upheld in England the cause of liberty. "During the century which followed the Revolution, the inclination of an English Protestant to trample on the Irishry was generally proportioned to the zeal which he professed for political liberty in the abstract. If he uttered any expression of compassion for the majority oppressed by the minority, he might be safely set down as a bigoted Tory and a High Churchman[3]".

[1] 29 Car. II. c. 3. An exception was made in the Statute, of leases under 3 years with a rent of two-thirds value, and assignments were ordered to be in writing unless of copyhold or custom-ary interest.

[2] Dean Swift, *The Presbyterian's Plea of Merit*, quoted by Macaulay, Vol. II. p. 295, note.

[3] Ib. p. 296.

CHAPTER VI.

The Land and the People.

It has been seen that the undoubted rights in the soil possessed by the free tribesman were recognised by Sir John Davies, but these rights had been completely swept away by the various revolutionary settlements and re-settlements of the land. That in a certain sense the English were justified after the time of Cromwell in looking upon Ireland as conquered territory, in which the possessory rights of the natives had been forfeited completely by their repeated risings against the English power, is undoubtedly true. Even the most ardent partisans of the cause of historical tenant-right admit the force of the legal objections to its existence; but they take another ground and say that the storm of war raged over the heads of an unmoved peasantry, who, when the storm has rolled by, are found still in their place unmindful of the change of ruler, and riveted to the land. There appears no reason whatever to believe this view to be correct. Those who know the Celtic character can understand how, in the war of race against race, the lowest earth-tiller would have felt stirred to rise against the national enemy.

The statements of Sir William Petty in his *Political Anatomy of Ireland*, it is true, seem to show the existence of the earth-tillers after the Cromwellian conquest much as before; but this proves nothing. The battle over, the cause lost, the earth-tiller returned to his holding because it was the only place he had to go to, and because no state to which the victorious enemy could reduce him could be more terrible than his natural condition. It presupposes no great amount of sagacity to imagine him capable of understanding that, whatever ruin might overtake the leaders of the lost cause, the 'hewers of wood and drawers of water' were too necessary a part of the social system for the conqueror, who needed their services, to drive them from the land. The survey of Sir William Petty recognised and thus in a sense legalised the possessory rights of the earth-tillers, and to as great an extent as this was done they could claim in the future to be regarded as having acknowledged rights in the soil. The Acts of Settlement, however, again unhinged all existing rights[1], and not only swept away any legal claims possible on the part of the lowest tenants, but also interrupted any growth of customary rights. Up to the dates of the Penal and Commercial Codes the wrongs of Ireland are mainly to be found in that injustice which is inseparable from the 'vae victis' of war. The history of the gravest wrongs of the native race begins from this period.

The suppression of Irish manufactures, and the endeavours to stamp out the creed and to reduce to a minimum the established proprietary rights of native holders in the land, resulted in throwing on the soil for support the bulk of the native race in the position of mere tenants at will. Given the existence of these masses of precarious holders tied to the soil, and bound generation after generation to its culture, it is strange that mere lapse of time did not establish customary tenures, and that as the years rolled on the tenant at will did not evolve into the customary holder. In English copyhold, at any rate according to the legal theory[2] of the origin of copyhold rights, the growth of these rights of the servile class in the land can be traced from a starting point of which complete slavery and unlimited personal services, combined with a mere usufruct by favour, are the characteristics, to the point where the services are limited specifically and absorbed in a money

---

[1] Sir William Petty estimated the superficies of Ireland at 10,500,000 Irish acres, of which 7,500,000 were good land, the rest being moor, bog, and lake. In 1641 the lands of the Church and of the Protestant owners amounted to about one-third of the good lands, the Catholics owning the remaining two-thirds. In 1672 he calculated that the possessions of the Church and of the Protestants amounted to 5,140,000 acres. The Catholics holding about half this quantity. Hallam, Vol. II. p. 392 (note).

[2] See ante, p. 33.

rent, and finally to the realization of freedom and determinate possessory rights[1]. Degraded as was the position of the Irish earth-tiller in the period following the accession of William the Third to the throne of England, it was in no way so desperate as the condition of the villeins of a Saxon manor over whom at the Conquest a Norman lord came to rule. The Saxon and the Norman, like the Irish and the English, present the spectacle of a conquered race settled on the land of their birth, but ruled by the stranger conqueror. In the former case not less than in the latter, sentiments of national hatred would tend to make the conqueror an oppressor, and the Norman yoke was heavy exceedingly : yet slowly but surely the villein established his rights in the soil, while the Irish peasant remained a precarious holder. The villein cultivator of the lord's demesne was but little in status above the mere beast of the field. Unable to leave the land without the lord's permission, if he ran away or was purloined he could be recovered by action ; holding his land at first at the unfettered will of the lord, by the meanest services, uncertain both in time and quantity ; prohibited from acquiring property, and liable if he even allowed the marriage of his daughter without the lord's permission to an action for damages for purloining property ; could a more debased condition be possible ? Yet he reached security of tenure. The express or implied manumission by the lord, the growth of the customary rights in the holding, and the recognition of his title by the manorial courts, built him by slow degrees a fortress against unjust exactions and summary ejectments. There is no trace of a similar growth of proprietary rights in the case of the Irish tenant at will.

It is often urged by the advocates of tenant-right in Ireland that the salvation of Irish land would have been the widespread application of the manorial system, and it is too frequently forgotten that the rights of the precarious holders in a manor cannot be established by Act of Parliament, but have their origin in long user, and the recognition of customs by the manorial courts. The plan has been tried in many cases in Ireland as far as it is possible to create newly a system,

---

[1] See *Commons and Common Fields*, T. E. Scrutton, p. 7.

the very essence of which is established custom. The large grants made by Henry the Second[1] were grants of Counties Palatine carrying all the rights of the creation of manorial courts; and Tipperary was also granted as a County Palatine to the Earl of Ormonde by Edward the Third. Again by 16 Car. I. c. 33, s. 9, confirmed by 21 & 22 Geo. III. c. 48 (Irish), every person having an allotment of lands of a specified extent was empowered to create a manor[2]: while upon the settlement of the escheated counties in Ulster, and generally in the grants of land made in the reign of James the First, the creation of manors was allowed, and the holding of Courts Baron authorized. Many of the undertakers did create manors, the law permitting them to enfeoff tenants to hold of themselves (unlike the law in England) provided they did not so aliene more than a moiety of their allotment. The absence of the growth of customary rights among the precarious tenants must therefore be ascribed not to the want of the manorial system, but to the fact that even in such a system the proprietary rights of the servile class can only be attained by long custom, not created instantly. The constant surge of change in the occupation of the land caused by the compulsory removals, whether by arbitrary evictions or by evictions for non-payment of rent, prevented the possibility of the acquisition of such rights by long user. The curse of absentee owners is responsible in a great measure for that total want amongst the lowest tenants of continuity in their holdings, which prevented the growth of customary rights. That such rights would have arisen in the natural course of events, had even the semblance of that consideration which always springs from personal relationships been present, is clear. In Ulster

---

[1] See p. 44 ante, and refer to Roll of King's Council in Ireland 16 Ric. II., where a petition to the king from the Lord Justice and Council of Ireland says "Les Franchises grantez in Ire-lande, que sont regale, tieles come Duresme et Cestre, vous oustont si bien de les grantez profitez come de grant partie de obeisance des persones en-fraunchies, et en chescune Fraunchise est Chauncellerie, Chequier, et conis-sance des Plees si bien de la corone come autres communes, et grantont auxint Chartres de Pardon." *The Chronicles and Memorials of Great Britain and Ireland during the Middle Ages.*

[2] *Law of Landlord and Tenant in Ireland.* J. S. Furlong, Vol. I. introd. p. 15.

customary rights arose, so universal as to lead eventually to their formal recognition by the Legislature. The greatest wrongs inflicted over most of Ireland by the landlords upon the tenants were the deeds which prevented such a continuity of possession as would have fostered customary traits. The Parliamentary persecution of Ireland acted upon the land system even more disastrously by its indirect methods than by its deliberate land legislation. The different Acts repressive of Irish manufactures resulted in making sheep breeding, in conjunction with an immense smuggling traffic in wool, the most profitable use to which Irish land could be put. The creation of the extensive tracts of pasturage[1] necessary for the grazing farms entailed the eviction of great numbers of small holders. The lands were often in the hands of middle-men, and no trace of consideration for the position of the small tenantry was shown. The absentee owners also pressed their agents to obtain the utmost value from the land, and so far was the grazing system carried that, despite the remonstrance of the Irish Parliament, covenants restricting the breaking or plough-ing of the soil, were introduced in the leases of the larger tenantry[2].

The effect of this mode of dealing with the land soon became apparent ; the limitation of the supply of plough-lands forced rents unnaturally high, with the effect that the Irish tenant, to whom land was a necessity, undertook to pay more than he was able. " The tenant was ruined by his liability to a charge out of all proportion to what the land could naturally produce, at any rate for a continued period, and the landlord became embarrassed by bankrupt tenants." How the tenant's hand was forced until an unnatural rent was offered is well shown by an allusion made in a remonstrance sent by the Northern Protestants to the Government in 1772, and quoted by Mr Justice Field[3]; "when the tenant's lease was ended they (the landlords) published in the newspapers that such a

---

[1] The creation of pasturage was further fostered by the fact that by the Tithe Agistment Act, 1735, pasture land was exempted from tithe. This Act was not repealed till 1823. (4 Geo. IV. c. 99, s. 35).

[2] See Field, pp. 267 and 268.

[3] Ibid. p. 270, note.

parcel of land was to be let, and that proposals in writing would
be received for it. They invited every covetous, envious and
malicious person to offer for his neighbour's possessions and
improvements. The tenant, knowing he must be the highest
bidder or turn out he knew not whither, would offer more than
the value. If he complained to the landlord that it was too dear,
the landlord answered that he knew it was so, but as it was in
a trading country the tenant must make up the deficiency by
his own industry." The diminution in the employment of
labour caused by the substitution of grazing for tillage inflicted
great misery, and we begin in the doings of the 'Houghers' in
Connaught to be confronted with one species of the agrarian
crime which has been so painfully prevalent in more recent
times.

The necessity of having at certain times a proportion of
Protestant tenants on the lands in order to insure the return to
Parliament of the landlord, also frequently led to the summary
ejectment of bodies of Catholic small holders[1], and hence by
destroying existing tenancies prevented the acquisition of any
customary rights. Again in the manner in which the enclosure of
commons was carried on (generally with a view to increasing the
grazing lands of the landlord) is to be found a frequent source
of loss, and hence of probable ejection from his holding, to the
tenant. For example, in Munster the excessive rents asked by
the landlords had been compensated by extensive grants of
commonage, yet in many cases these commons were unscrupulously enclosed and not the slightest reduction in rents
made[2]. In a greater or less degree every imposition which
burdened the tenant, or which aggravated the repellent feeling
of landlord and tenant, tended to prejudice the latter's chance
of security in his holding.

A prominent place among the forces of social disunion was
taken by the tithe question. The payment of tithes was a great
burden on the Irish peasant[3], and embittered the relations

[1] Notice a petition presented by the
Catholics in January, 1793.

[2] Sigerson, p. 128.

[3] "Fitzgibbon, afterwards Earl of
Clare, stated in 1786 in the House that

he had known as many as 120 processes
for tithes to be going on at the same
time in the county of Limerick against
poor tenants." Field, p. 276.

inter se of owner and occupier. Not only must it have seemed a hardship to the tenant to find the scanty fruits of his labour trenched upon for the support of a church which he abhorred, but also the fact that the great grazing estates of the large owners were exempt from this imposition[1], must have seemed a most deliberate wrong. The tenant would keenly resent the fact that in Ulster the Protestant tenantry had succeeded in freeing themselves largely from this burden by the assertion of customs of exemption with regard to certain crops, for example, potatoes and flax, while he remained bound: and the modern history of Wales has taught the practical impossibility of impressing on the mind of the tenant that the tithe is a charge on the land and had already been considered when the rent was fixed. The Irish tithes in addition were almost always sold by the incumbents and passed into the hands of the tithe-farmers while the 'canting' of tithes was also resorted to[2].

During the first half of the eighteenth century the Protestant ascendency was unbroken in the higher grades of the Irish social system, but as time passed the very completeness of this sovereignty led to a relaxation of some of the crushing burdens piled upon the Catholics. The Penal Code was allowed to rust, and some degree of common interests sprung up between the two religions. There was a marked increase in those infallible signs of the prosperity of a community, the making of buildings, and the investment of money in the development of land. Unfortunately the improvement was strictly confined to the higher grades of society; the English and Catholic landlords showed signs of a rapprochement, but the landlord and the tenant showed none. Even the relaxations of the Commercial Code became evils to the agricultural tenant by extending the amount of lands devoted to grazing. Agrarian troubles reached a crisis. The Levellers, who at first had limited their attempts to the forcible prevention of the enclosing of common lands[3], became a serious disturbing element

---

[1] By the Tithe Agistment Act, 1735, repealed 4 Geo. IV. c. 99, s. 35.

[2] *Two Centuries of Irish History*, edited by Prof. Bryce, p. 65.

[3] See Sigerson, p. 128, quoting "An enquiry into the causes of the outrages committed by the Levellers or Whiteboys," 1762.

to the community, when, under the name of Whiteboys, they perpetrated outrages which were a menace to the peace of the country, and which were obviously aimed at the destruction of the whole of the existing system of landlord and tenant. The rising of the Oak Boys[1] in 1763 was originally directed against excessive road corvees, but afterwards took, like the Whiteboy rising, the form of general resistance to exactions, rack rents, and other features of the oppressive land system. These outbreaks, really the result of utter misery, were almost wantonly misunderstood by the Government, and arbitrary repressive Acts were passed. It was argued that the outbreaks were concocted in the French interest, and no attempt was made to investigate the true origin of the risings or to remedy the social evils which gave them birth. In 1771 came the Association of the "Hearts of Steel[2]," an organization produced by a set of circumstances typical of the manner in which Irish estates were managed by absentee owners. When the leases on a certain estate expired, the owner suddenly demanded large fines on renewal from his tenants; these not being forthcoming the lands passed into the hands of a group of speculators, and a wholesale eviction, whereby the tenants lost not only their homesteads but also the value of their improvements, followed. When too a body of Catholic tenantry was established under these speculators (for in the case alluded to the ejected tenants were Protestants) their position was most miserable; for the middlemen, who had paid the fine and taken up the leases as a speculation solely for profit, were men "who not content with moderate interest for their money, racked the tenants to a pitch beyond the reach of the old tenants[3]."

[1] Sigerson, p. 130.

[2] Both the "Oak Boys" and the "Hearts of Steel" were exclusively *Protestant* organizations: this is a remarkable proof that the struggle between nation and nation, or creed and creed, was rapidly changing to a class war between landlord and tenant.

[3] Among the many grievances advanced by the "Hearts of Steel" in their petition to the Government, particular stress was laid on the exaction of the county cess: it would appear that the cause of their complaint in this case was not so much the amount of the exaction as the fact that it was often misappropriated, and used by those whom they held to be tyrants for their private advantage. See Field, p. 277.

In 1757 the Duke of Bedford had promised to abridge the penal laws, and to a large extent their rigour had been lessened as regards the Catholic gentry ; but the position of the Catholic peasant remained unaltered, and the land law was a terrible burden. Bad as was the position of the Protestant small holder, that of the Catholic was worse; they shared in common the evils of a system in which the landlord was all powerful, but the Catholic was burdened with additional preventives to the possession of a secure interest in the land. The hereditary sentiment which bound the native race to Ireland being wanting in the case of the Protestant settlers, masses of the Protestant tenantry, as had been the case earlier[1], abandoned the land, which seemed under a curse, and emigrated to America. At length a slight amelioration of the case of the Catholic tenants was effected by an Act of 1771[2], by which under certain stringent conditions they were allowed to undertake the reclamation of bog-land. In 1775 the American war broke out, and reacted upon Irish affairs by causing a relaxation of the fetters in which the country had so long been bound. A really useful Act was passed in 1778[3] enabling the Irish to take leases for 999 years or five lives[4]. It is to be feared, however, that the origin of this Act lay not so much in consideration for the sufferings of the Catholic tenantry[5] as because the landlords found that unless some security of tenure was granted it was hopeless to expect the tenant to improve the soil. In 1779 came the repeal of the Restriction Acts, and but for the trade jealousy of England the Commercial Code would have been wholly repealed. This course was really necessary, for the war with America had closed the chief marts for Irish goods, and more misery and discontent was added to Ireland's already brimming cup.

The weakness of England was Ireland's opportunity. In 1782 Grattan, backed by the volunteers (which the exigencies of England during her American war had compelled her to allow Ireland to organize for self-defence), succeeded in gaining

---

[1] During the oppression of the Protestant party by Tyrconnel. Ante, p. 83.

[2] 11 & 12 Geo. III. c. 21 (Irish).

[3] 17 & 18 Geo. III. c. 49 (Irish).

[4] See Sigerson, pp. 132—134.

[5] This was, however, the year of the Catholic Relief Bill.

an Independent Parliament, and obtained the repeal of Poyning's Act. Legislative freedom, however, brought no benefit to the radical evils of the land system, though commerce and manufacture relieved from restraint grew and increased prodigiously. The fact that the peasantry were deeply imbued, and with reason, with the idea that the influence of the laws was exerted solely in favour of the landlords, operated largely to defeat even beneficent legislation. Long leases were frequently granted after the Acts of Settlement, but these passing exclusively into the hands of middlemen and never direct to the tenants, only aggravated the evils of their position. The law of distress also was by itself enough to fix for ever in their minds the idea that the landlord was an unjust taskmaster, and the law his complaisant helpmeet. The remedy of distress was indeed recognized by the Brehon Law to the fullest degree, in fact it may be considered to have been the universal mode of procedure for the recovery of any claim ; and the Senchus Mor with its provisions for notice to the defendant, for the 'stay,' and for a near equivalent to replevin, shows a highly elaborate system. In two ways, however, it completely differed from the English law of distress, (1) the remedy was entirely extra-judicial, and (2) it was applicable (resembling in this the Teutonic distress) to all cases and not merely to certain specified classes of claims[1]. The feudal law of distress undoubtedly developed into a powerful weapon for the landlord. When there was a difference between him and the tenant, he was able as feudal superior to seize the tenant's goods; the Common Law rule that the goods so seized could not be sold was supplemented by a statute giving this power, and a further Act enabled him to seize growing crops[2]. The tenant's rights con-

---

[1] The late Sir Henry Maine pointed out that this last fact opened a wide field for probable injustice on the part of the English settlers to the native Irish, for the statutes which made an unlawful distress a capital felony would punish the native in many cases for using the only method for recovery of a claim with which he was acquainted.

Early Hist. of Inst., lecture x. ; see also quotation from Edmund Spenser there given.

[2] One of the recommendations of the Devon Commissioners was that this statute should be repealed and the costs of a distress strictly limited. The original theory of the feudal distress regarded it as a means of

sisted merely in a resort to the dangerous action of replevin which entailed his giving a bond with two responsible sureties, to double the value of the goods distrained, as security that he would prosecute the suit with effect and without delay. It was the gradual amendment of the law in favour of the tenant, by imposing the observance of many legal technicalities (with an accompanying penalty as to a trespasser ab initio) on the distrainor, which led to a later stage of the Irish land history when, on account of the legal difficulties involved, the process of distress was adopted as a last resource by the landlord[1].

In the past century the most patent evils of the land system had been the frequent changes of tenancy in the small holdings and the not unfrequent blotting out of large numbers of such holdings, which prevented the peasant from attaining any security of tenure by the growth of customary rights. A new phase of the land question was now entered upon, insecurity of tenure still marked the small Irish holdings but instead of a tendency to unduly restrict their number they were created with a most disastrous prodigality. The immense cultivation of the potato, Raleigh's 'fatal gift,' brought the most terrible attendant evils. Easy of cultivation, and requiring but small plots of land for its production in large quantities, it fostered an increase of population entirely out of proportion to the land to which it looked for its exclusive support. The famine of 1739 brought no lesson to the improvident peasantry, and the commercial developments of 1782 to 1800 did not aid the case of the small agricultural holders.

The desire of the landlords for political influence[2] led them to increase the number of the small holdings to such an extent that, considered with regard to its effect on the agricultural

---

compelling the performance of the feudal services, and did not contemplate such a case as the recovery of rent, therefore the goods of the tenant might by the Statute of Marlbridge be merely retained as a pledge and not sold. Richey, *Irish Land Laws*, p. 40.

[1] Ib. p. 40.

[2] Before the Reform Act many of the counties were absolutely subservient to the landlord interest. *Inst. of English Government*, Homersham Cox, p. 108. Lord Farnborough's *Constitutional History*, Vol. I. p. 298.

system, the Acts of 1771, 1778 and 1782 which enabled Catholics to hold land, and the Act of 1793 which granted them the 40s. franchise, must be looked upon as evils despite their manifest equity of principle. The small holdings created for the purpose of securing a weighty tenant vote were let at rents exceeding their true worth, owing to the increase in the value of land caused by war prices, and the small freeholder was at once, upon prices regaining their normal level, involved in difficulties; whilst the landlord on his part, despite the provisions of the Eviction Act 1816[1] and the Subletting Act 1826[2], was burdened by bankrupt tenants. The following table will illustrate the rapid growth of the small freeholds, caused by the desire for political influence felt by the landlords, and the avid eagerness of the Irish peasantry for small holdings.

FREEHOLDS, 1795—1830[3].

	40s.	£20	£50	Total
1795	4,768	408	344	5,520
1796	64,752	5,109	3,195	73,056
1803	157,159	10,096	7,009	174,264
1821	184,229	15,139	11,066	210,431
1828	191,732	6,806	18,369	216,907
1830	14,246	7,639	17,819	39,704

After the abolition in 1829[4] of the 40s. freehold suffrage, the tenancies mostly took the form of tenancies from year to year; for the rise in the value of land, which had been caused by the outbreak of the French war and the depreciation of the currency, had been followed by a subsequent depression, and the landlords had realized the fact that under a lease by which a certain rent was reserved they reaped no benefit from an increase in the value of land, while a fall invariably involved them in the losses of the tenant. For the same reason they sought to

[1] 56 Geo. III. c. 88.
[2] 7 Geo. IV. c. 29.
[3] Taken from the statistical article
on Ireland in *Encyc. Brit.* by Mr T. F. Henderson.
[4] 10 Geo. IV. c. 8.

consolidate their interest, and large clearances were the result of a desire to substitute large farms for small holdings. This is alluded to as a necessary evil in the report of the Select Committee of the House of Commons in 1830[1]. Leases were, however, still sometimes granted from political motives until the uncertainty of the tenant vote and the extension of the suffrage in 1850 by 13 & 14 Vict. c. 69 to the occupiers of land of the annual rating of £12 extinguished this cause for their creation.

[1] After 1838, on account of the burden of the poor laws many small holdings were abolished and large farms substituted.

CHAPTER VII.

IRELAND FROM 1800 TO 1850.

IRISH legislative independence failed to produce those golden results which were hoped for from it, and the brief period of its existence calls for little notice. Cases of individual patriotism stand out against a background of general corruption, and the wit and eloquence of Ireland glitter with that seductive charm which they unfortunately associate with no commensurate result. The advantages gained by the increased commerce and manufacturing successes of the nation were more than counterbalanced by the immense increase of population which rose from 2,845,932 in 1785 to 5,356,594 in 1803. The failure of Ireland to govern herself was due to many causes. Noticeably, the unwise policy of the leaders of the people who encouraged the anti-English feeling, and the wild surge of disappointed passions in a people who had expected a millennium and were tortured perpetually with new hopes of increased freedom, which vanished as soon as seen. Secret societies were formed, and that worst side of the Celtic character, which would attain its end whatever the means used may be, became prominent. The lawless example of France, and the real misery of the agricultural population, bore fruit. In 1798 rebellion broke out, in the form of a murderous revolt organized and set on foot by the 'United Irishmen.' Union with England was now unavoidable ; taught again the lesson that concession to Ireland was merely regarded as weakness, England took the reins into her own hands.

By whatever means the Union was carried (and the means employed were far from meritorious) it was undoubtedly at this time the only alternative to complete separation, and the Union of 1801[1] was probably for Ireland, and certainly for England, the best step that could have been taken. It was signalized, however, by no improvement in the strained relations of the land classes in Ireland, and causes were at work tending to again rain havoc on the peasants. The passing of the Union withdrew to England a still greater portion of the landowning class, and absenteeism[2] became the rule; while the expenditure and extravagance of the Irish landlords was increased by their being brought into contact with the wealthy landlords of England, and with a society which normally lived above its resources. The class of middlemen which absenteeism fostered were utterly wanting in feeling for the needs of the agricultural tenant, and regarded them solely in the light of a rent-paying machine; while, as has been said, the rise in prices caused by the French war produced an increase in the value of the land, so that leases were taken by the tenants at exorbitant rents.

The increase of population continued with terrible rapidity, in 1841 it reached 8,175,124, in 1845 nearly nine millions[3], and the whole nation were competitors for the land. This, as has been shown, together with the cultivation of the potato, which made minute subdivisions of the land possible, and the readiness of the landlords to grant small holdings from political motives, settled on the land a load of peasant tenants which it was completely unable to support, save in a time of exceptional prosperity. The nature of the holdings thus created is well described by Mr Shaw Lefevre, who says " throughout a great part of the West and South of Ireland, every facility was given to the letting of lands in small holdings of from half an acre up to five or six acres. On taking possession the

---

[1] Act of Union 1800, 39 & 40 Geo. III. c. 67.

[2] A very curious proof of how early the evils of absenteeism began to be felt in Ireland is given by the following extract from The Black Book of Holy Trinity Church, Dublin, 26 Edw. I. (1297) quoted by Sir William Betham in his Constitutions of England and Ireland, p. 265, "Magnates and others also, who dwell in England, or elsewhere out of this land, and draw the profits of their lands out of this country, and send nothing for the preservation of their holdings, or their tenants' security, shall etc."

[3] Field, p. 282.

tenant would himself build a mud hut at little cost; a few weeks of labour sufficed for preparing the land for potatoes, digging the crop, and cutting turf for fuel from the common bog; the rent was usually paid in labour and the spare time was spent in fishing, or in work at a distance. The general social condition of this class was as low as it is possible to conceive. They constituted nearly half the population of Ireland, and, with rare exceptions, lived in cabins with one room only, which they often shared with their pigs. There was no inducement to them to improve their condition, either from a healthy competition with their neighbours, or from a sense of security in their holdings[1]".

The depression of prices in 1816 and the following years brought financial troubles not only upon the peasant class, but also upon the landlords who had entered upon extravagant modes of living, calculated upon the false basis of the apparently high rent-roll of their estates; a purely fancy sum produced by unlimited competitive demand and limited supply. The rents, which had doubled in thirty years, melted at once on the normal balance of value being reached: still such was the demand for peasant holdings that, whatever might prove ultimately to be the solvency of the candidates, no landlord found a difficulty in letting his land even at a high rent.

The agricultural tenants being thus eager to obtain the land, the nature of the tenure granted them was naturally regulated by the wishes of the landlord class, and these were almost universally swayed by the desire for political influence. Until 1829, when the annual value was raised to ten pounds, a freehold rated at 40s. was the qualification for a vote, hence until the Reform Act a freehold became the general estate granted; but it was a freehold of the smallest possible kind, viz. an estate for life only, and it is apparent that such a tenure was absolutely hostile to any chance of improvement in the soil or to any agricultural development of the holdings. Indeed it may be considered that the tenants were only in a technical sense freeholders, the landlord's influence over them being scarcely less than that exercised over the tenants from year to

---

[1] *Peel and O'Connell*, Rt. Hon. G. Shaw Lefevre, p. 257.

year, as by keeping a 'hanging gale' over them he could, by
the threat of demanding immediate payment, prejudice their
position[1].

Leaseholds for terms of years were then granted, but this
tenure became unpopular with the landlords[2], and as political
motives ceased to influence the lettings (for the tenantry were
often avowedly hostile to the landlord's political party) the
small holdings came to be held largely either (1) from year
to year or (2) at will, and after the Act of 1850[3] this practice
became almost universal.

Tenancies from year to year, which for some curious reason
the Irish tenants have always regarded as a species of tenancy
in perpetuity, dated from the reign of Henry the Eighth, when
Potkyn's case[4] first gave them legal recognition. In several
ways the development of this system of letting is interesting.
Until the reign of George the Third it could only be founded
either on express agreement, or upon implication arising from
the acts of the parties or from the payment of rent; for the
doubt as to what mode of tenancy should be implied when the
letting did not specify it, was held to be decided on the ground
of the mode of letting most common at the time of the creation
of the tenancy. This was held to be tenancy at will until the
time of Lord Mansfield, and as regards tenancies created after
that date, from year to year[5]. At first these tenancies were
created by an express demise for one year, and then from year
to year as long as both parties desired, at an annual rent.
They can now be created in this way, but when this is the
case can only be terminated at the end of the second year of
holding, or, if the tenancy has continued longer than this, then
by the ordinary methods for determining an estate from year to
year[6].

---

[1] *Peel and O'Connell*, G. Shaw Lefevre, p. 104.

[2] See ante, page 100. It was stated
before the Bessborough Committee that
the tenantry also were averse to the
idea of long terms, holding that they
were a derogation of their rights in the
soil and preferred a year to year tenancy, which they regarded as unlimited
in extent.

[3] See ante, p. 101.

[4] *Year Book*, 14 Hen. VIII. fol. 10.

[5] Timmons *v.* Rowlinson, 3 Burr
1603. Shore *v.* Porter, 3 T. R. 13.

[6] Furlong's *Landlord and Tenant*,
Vol. I. Intro. p. 35.

The most usual form of these tenancies in modern times was where they were implied without the existence of a written agreement from the payment of rent. This tenure was always looked upon by the tenants as being practically in perpetuity, and under it they would at least to a certain extent improve the lands, which it was almost impossible to induce them to do under tenures for a term of years. They considered a holding for a term certain to be an invasion of their rights in the soil, and on the termination of such lettings returned the land 'run out.' It is evident that this tenancy from year to year was capable of grave abuses; the landlord, by serving a notice to quit, could compel the tenant either to surrender his holding and abandon the improvements he had made, or pay an increased rent. Only too frequently this plan was adopted, and it had the invariable result of causing the tenant to accept the higher rent, the ultimate consequence of which was his ruin and eviction.

A mistake frequently made in speaking of these tenures was pointed out by the late Dr Richey[1], namely, the statement that the tenant had no right to sell or sublet to whom he pleased. The origin of the mistake arises in the fact that the tenant could pass no greater estate than rested in him, that is merely the term of the year, at the end of which the tenancy, unless the landlord consented to the new tenant, determined. It is therefore obvious that save with the consent of the landlord no very valuable estate in the land could be passed. This was undoubtedly considered a wrong by the tenants who, considering their holdings in the light of a perpetuity, could not comprehend the apparent restraint upon alienation.

Tenancies at will, amounting in result to a holding only for as long as the landlord pleased, were not as common as those from year to year; for as will be seen from what has been said relative to the yearly tenancies, a tenancy at will could only be created in modern times by express agreement, or implied where the circumstances of the case preclude the possibility of a tenancy from year to year having been contemplated.

[1] *Irish Land Laws*, p. 38.

Under the influence of a certain set of causes the history of the small holdings has been traced from 1800 to 1850. It has been seen that the number of these holdings increased largely, and that their tenure, at first generally that of freeholds for life, became changed to a system of tenancy from year to year. But during this epoch many other causes were at work as well, and other and most potent circumstances were widening the breach between landlord and tenant, and were desolating the unhappy kingdom. Protestant omnipotence had been rudely shaken; the agitation of O'Connell and the efforts of the priests had roused from the torpor of despair the passions of the Celtic race; concessions such as the Catholic emancipation had been wrung from unwilling masters, not freely given; the money obtained from rents which ground the tenant holders to the dust for the most part passed out of the country to a clique of owners, alien in race and religion; while bitterness of feeling was fomented by the fact that after 1838, to free themselves from the burden of the poor laws, the landlords in many cases abolished the small holdings and created large farms. In order to do this, and in order to compel the payment of rents which were really beyond the powers of the small holders, the landlords employed that machinery of the law which at this time could always be relied on to aid their class. In 1816 an Eviction Act had been passed, and gigantic "clearances" became the rule. The small holders were driven in crowds from the homes to which they were bound by a hundred ties of old association and tradition, which they regarded as their inalienable property, and the value of which was mainly owing to the improvements they had themselves made[1]. Such associa-

---

[1] "It is admitted on all hands, that according to the general practice in Ireland, .the landlord builds neither dwelling-house nor farm offices, nor puts fences, gates, etc. into good order before he lets his land to a tenant. The cases when a landlord does any of these things are the exception. The system of giving aid in these matters is becoming more prevalent. In most cases whatever is done in the way of building or fencing is done by the tenant, and in the ordinary language of the country, dwelling-houses, farm buildings and even the making of fences are described by the general words 'improvements,' which is thus employed to denote the necessary adjuncts to a farm, without which, in England or Scotland, no tenant would be found to rent it." *Report of the Devon Commissioners*, p. 1122. It is

tions as the Ribbonmen are not produced without a feeling of intense class hatred; and complete alienation of thought and sympathy between the dominant and the servient class prevailed.

Just at the time when this antagonism was most marked; when the peasants, ejected from their holdings in vast numbers, became the movers in every species of agrarian combination; when the absolute destitution that prevailed amongst the lower ranks of the people drove them to complete dependence on the potato for food, and made cultivation of it by every poverty-stricken squatter the sole sustenance of his household; when continued bad times had dissipated any shadow of that reserve fund which the improvident peasant so rarely laid by, the food which was the very life of the nation, failed.

This failure, partial in 1845 and complete in 1846, brought famine with fever in its train, and death dark-winged brooded over the face of the land. Misery and despair seized the people, and horrors unimaginable crowd the history of the terrible year that turned the country into one vast grave. No words can paint the scenes that were the every day history of that time. The clarion had been sounded however, class prejudice, religious antagonism, national differences, were lost for the while. England rose to help the dying and to fight as far as lay in her power the inexorable forces of starvation and disease. From the cot and from the castle the wealth of England was poured in no scanty stream to succour and sustain. Alas, the magnitude of the awful crisis was far beyond the power of hurried organization and defective plans to cope with, even though into the lap of the perishing nation was flung the riches of a mighty kingdom. Public works on a gigantic basis were schemed, but the starving people dropped dead as they worked, labour and exposure being fatal; and the plan, which had developed into a mass of jobbery, was abandoned. Re-

notable in contrast to the above that as early as the reign of William III. compensation for permanent improvements was given to the Protestant ecclesiastics, for 10 Will. III. c. 6 (Irish) enabled every ecclesiastical dignitary to recover from his successor two-thirds of the money laid out on necessary improvements. See Sigerson, pp. 108 —110.

course was then had to large supplies of food rations; but despite all efforts 200,000 to 300,000 perished of famine or disease.

When the ghastly picture is considered, one is filled with surprise that the efforts of England—which, though they came late in the day and were deficient in their modes of application, yet represented a large-hearted generosity and a national sympathy with distress which should have appealed strongly to the Celtic character—were not the basis of a bond of union between the two nations. Had a permanent understanding been built up on the basis of this stupendous catastrophe one would (bearing in mind the miserable history of crime and bloodshed caused by the antagonism of race and creed) have hesitated to call it dearly bought even at the price of so appalling a sacrifice of life. Alas, the breach was widened rather than bridged, the lack of gratitude shown by the Irish people further prejudiced English opinion against them.

This forgetfulness of deep obligations is strange, for the facts appeal strongly even to very prejudiced critics. Mr Sullivan in his *New Ireland* says, "Even the dark cloud of Irish famine had its silver lining. If it is painful to recall the disastrous errors of irresolution and panic, one can linger gratefully over memories of Samaritan philanthropy, of efficacious generosity, of tenderest sympathy. The people of England behaved nobly....From every considerable town in England there poured subscriptions, amounting in the aggregate to hundreds of thousands of pounds[1]." Again speaking of the resident landlords he says, "No adequate tribute has ever been paid to the memory of those Irish landlords—and they were men of every party and creed—who perished martyrs to duty in that awful time; who did not fly the plague-reeking workhouse or fever-tainted court. Their names would make a goodly roll of honour[2]"; and he further pays a well-deserved tribute to the courage and humanity displayed by many of the Protestant clergy.

Events have proved nevertheless that the severance between

---

[1] Vol. I. p. 139.   [2] Vol. I. p. 133 (note).

landlord and tenant was even more complete after the famine
than before, and as the critical complications of the land system
are in the main due to the absence of sympathy between the
two classes, it is important to notice the reasons which caused
the Irish people to look on the famine as a slaughter for which
the English were responsible. That in a great measure this
was owing to the unscrupulous misrepresentation of political
agitators, and to the readiness of the peasant class to ascribe
their misfortunes to any cause rather than their own impro-
vidence, is true; but it was partially also the result of minor
concurrent errors on the part of England which, placed in the
scale of national animosity, outweighed all the self-sacrifice
and generosity displayed by her. The regulation which made
the surrender of land a condition precedent to poor law relief;
the breakdown of the poor law system, an event neither remarkable nor culpable seeing that it was but newly established
and quite unsuited to wrestle with such an unforeseen and
gigantic calamity; the evictions and clearances which had
turned thousands from their homes; the 'famine clearances'
(rendered necessary from the landlord's point of view by the
fact that the destitute peasantry were unable to find means to
till the soil, and that rent paying was the exception); and the
opposition in England to many of the plans for free ports and
abolition of duties[1], assumed to the Irish, seeking eagerly for
some blamable person on whom to lavish the bitter wrath
that their miseries had raised in them, the shape of crimes of
terrible magnitude.

The passion and prejudice of the Celt again flung itself in
wild fury against the dominant class. Emigration, which entailed great hardships, followed the famine, and not less than
two millions of the population were scattered over the face of
the earth, principally in England and America. Fenianism
began to spread, originating amongst the Irish in America,
while revolt simmered constantly under the surface of Irish
politics at home. Twice it took head, once in the feeble and

---

[1] In reality this opposition was
purely owing to the party principles of
protection and free trade which were
then fighting the corn law battle
in England, the protectionists being
afraid of granting a precedent.

futile revolution of 1848 and again in the risings in 1867;
while plot and intrigue against the Government went on
unceasingly.

Even before the famine the fall of prices and the consequent failure of rents had involved a large number of the
landlords in financial difficulties. Estates were frequently
mortgaged up to the hilt and charged with every species of
incumbrance, and the expensive and complex procedure of the
Court of Chancery was found unsuited to meet the difficulties
presented by an attempted sale of estates so burdened; while
it was the only means by which an incumbrancer could proceed. The disadvantage of the system of incumbered estates
in the hands of absentee and unbusinesslike owners was per-
sistently pressed, and the substitution of practical men, who
would take personal concern in the paying development of
the land, and whose direct interest would be involved in making
permanent profit from their estates, urged; the aid of legislature was invoked, and an Act, 11 & 12 Vict. c. 48, known as
the Incumbered Estates Act, 1848, was passed.

The purpose aimed at cannot be better described than in
the words of Mr Gladstone, who in 1870, speaking of this Act,
said[1], "It had a most benevolent object; it was intended to
introduce capital into Ireland, to relieve impoverished proprietors of that country from that which was to them not a
privilege but a burden—the possession of land which they
could not rightly use or manage—and to transfer it into the
hands of a more vigorous and opulent race of proprietors with a
view to the development of the riches of the soil." The means
employed in this Act to produce these effects are best shown
by a reference to the Act itself. Section 2 enacted "that
where any land in Ireland shall be subject to any Incumbrance
it shall be lawful for the owner of such land to contract (subject
to the approval of the Court) for the sale thereof, freed from
all such Incumbrances, and such sale, if approved by the Court,
shall be carried into effect under the provisions of this Act;
and that any such owner, or any person being an incumbrancer

---

[1] Hansard, 3rd series, cxcix. p. 344.

on such land in possession of the Title Deeds and writings
relating thereto, without having so contracted, may apply
to the Court for the sale of such land under the provisions
of this Act[1]." The *modus operandi* of the Act was that
on payment into Court of the purchase money (which was
divided amongst the parties entitled according to their claims)
the purchaser received a parliamentary title free from incumbrances.

Large numbers of landlords whose estates were hopelessly
involved, and to whom the famine with its attendant failure of
rent and increase of taxation had brought ruin, flocked to the
Courts. By the end of 1858 there had been 8,300 conveyances,
and purchase money to the amount of twenty-three millions
had passed through the Court[2]; while so satisfactory was the
working of the Act, that in 1858 "The Irish Landed Estate
Act," 21 & 22 Vict. c. 72, extended the same principle even to
unincumbered estates. Constant applications have been made
under these Acts, until at the present time over £52,000,000
has been invested in the purchase of Irish land.

The class of landlord created by the purchases has not
been very satisfactory. The purely business element which
characterised the purchase of lands from the Court as a speculation, excluded any feeling of reciprocal obligations founded
on a bond of personal acquaintance as distinguished from legal
relations, and the 'new man' proved even more obnoxious to the
Irish peasant than the landlord to whose faults he was accustomed and with whose foibles he was acquainted. It is a
curious but undeniable trait of the Celtic character that even an
unjust landlord becomes in some sort hallowed by long association; while a new comer, unacquainted in all probability
with the curious turns of Irish character, gives mortal offence
and stirs up unending rancour by the doing of acts often both
beneficial and well meant, simply because his more businesslike
methods are not understood and his insistence on his rights is
considered a wrong.

[1] 11 & 12 Vict. c. 48, sec. 2.
[2] See Field, p. 285, "of this total, three millions came from English and other foreign purchasers, and twenty millions represented Irish capital in-vested in land."

The deep acquaintance with Irish character necessary to fully appreciate that while the peasants can be led to almost anything, they can be driven to nothing, was not likely to be found in the speculative purchaser of an estate; nor would he easily realise that in Ireland the ideas of justice and custom are inextricably mingled. Moreover the landlords of large estates are far more likely to deal liberally with their tenants than petty proprietors, and during the first eight years' working of the Incumbered Estates' Act, 3,197 estates passed into the hands of 7,216 purchasers.

On the other hand the more business-like characteristics of the new landlords, and the practical interest which they took in the cultivation of their lands, tended to largely increase the surface prosperity of Ireland; while the more reasonable system of agriculture rendered possible by the relief afforded to the land by the removal of the surplus population, and the thinned numbers of the destitute (for the famine had resulted in a literal 'survival of the fittest'), operated in the same direction. Wealth grew and expanded, railways were increased and extended, and facilities for connecting the producing districts with the centres of sale sprang up. Everywhere an apparent prosperity was presented which, though afterwards proved to be illusionary and to have rested on no firm basis, for the time being deceived even shrewd observers. The Irish agrarian troubles seemed things of the past, and the 'Young Ireland' and Fenian risings were neither very considerable nor attended with much important result.

The very causes, however, which were rendering the land more valuable, were but increasing the stakes for which landlord and tenant were playing. If the conflicting claims of the landlord's legal title and the tenant's (assumed) moral right had given rise to desperate bitterness of feeling even when only an acre holding and a mud hovel were at stake, naturally the passions were still more excited when interests of substantial value were concerned. The era too of Protestant ascendency had waned. The Catholic Church was now an institution of immense power. Exclusively interested in the tenant, it brought to bear against the landlord class the whole influence of organization, and became the binding force of the native element of disunion. The landlord grasped but more firmly at his rights when he felt the sceptre slipping from him, and under the smiling mask of order the two classes braced themselves for a struggle to the death.

PART III.

THE IRELAND OF TO-DAY.

CHAPTER VIII.

ULSTER TENANT-RIGHT AND THE DEVON COMMISSION.

IT has been shown that amongst the small holders in Ireland the system of tenure was, from various causes, almost exclusively reduced to a mere holding from year to year; and that under this system (despite the irradicable impression of the Irish peasantry that it amounted to a tenure in perpetuity) the landlord was able to crush out the tenant's interest in the land. It has been shown also that while all the improvements were the work of the occupier he neither acquired a secure interest in his holding, nor any right of compensation if the fruits of his labour were appropriated. In addition it has been pointed out that in the main part of Ireland no customary rights were acquired by the precarious holders. In Ulster, however, things were different, and almost from the time of the formation of the settlement in the reign of James the First, the Protestant tenantry began to rapidly thrive and prosper; whilst a customary usage, so widespread as finally to obtain the formal recognition of the Legislature[1], gradually developed.

The origin and spread of this Ulster tenant-right is both interesting and important in the history of Irish land law, and the custom has to many persons represented a system which, if extended throughout Ireland, would have solved the agrarian troubles. But as will be seen—though greatly preferable to the total insecurity of tenure prevalent in other parts of the country—it is in some ways unsatisfactory.

[1] See post, p. 140.

In 1843 Sir Robert Peel promised that a Royal Commission
should be appointed to examine the nature of the tenure of land
in Ireland, and on the 20th of November in that year the Commission accordingly issued, and was directed to five gentlemen
well acquainted with that country. The inquiry then conducted,
and known by the name of the Devon Commission, throws much
light on the nature of landed relations throughout Ireland,
and lays considerable stress on the existence and beneficial
working of the Ulster customs. Unfortunately no effort was
made to represent the tenant interest among the Commissioners
appointed, and the scheme was therefore at once attacked
as being purely in the interest of the landlord; O'Connell
remarking "you might as well consult butchers about keeping
Lent as consult these men about the rights of farmers[1]." Still,
despite the prejudice displayed against it, a most valuable
amount of evidence was collected, and had any immediate
legislative action been taken on the strength of the report
presented, it seems likely that commendable reforms might
have been instituted and much of the after troubles of the land
question avoided. The report is perhaps scarcely bold enough,
but it bears every trace of studied impartiality. It is of course
impossible to deal with it at length, but an examination of the
most notable points shows that the Commission recognized the
substantial justice of many of the claims for fixity of tenure[2],
and the crying need for a fair remuneration to the tenant
for the money and labour expended by him in permanent
improvements. The Commissioners rightly ascribed the undeniable evils existing in the land system to the alienation of
sympathy between landlord and tenant, and stated that "the
foundation of almost all the evils by which the social condition
of Ireland is disturbed, is to be traced to those feelings of
mutual distrust, which too often separate the classes of landlord and tenant, and prevent all united exertion for the common
benefit[3]."

The Devon Commission brought into great prominence the

---

[1] *Peel and O'Connell* by the Rt Hon.
Shaw Lefevre, p. 234.

[2] See *Digest of Evidence before*

Devon Commission, p. 1122.
[3] *Ibid.* p. 1166.

fact that the comparative quiescence of the north of Ireland, which contrasted strongly with the disturbed state of landed relations throughout the rest of the country, was due to the existence of the Ulster custom being generally 'either authorized or connived at by the landlord.' This custom of tenant-right—a thing at that time absolutely without the sanction of law—consisted of an assumed right on the part of the tenant to sell the goodwill of his holding subject to its rent. Such a custom was naturally regarded from different points of view by the landlord and the tenant. This is well illustrated by two definitions of tenant-right quoted by Mr Seebohm. The landlord defines it thus[1]; "tenant-right is a custom under which the tenant farmers in the north of Ireland—or, at all events, in those districts where the custom prevails—expect when they have occasion to give up their farms, that their landlords will allow them to obtain from the incoming tenant such a sum as shall remunerate them for their improvements upon those farms...and for the goodwill of the farm." From the standpoint of the tenant it is defined as follows; "tenant-right I consider to be the claim of the tenant and his heirs to continue in undisturbed possession of the farm so long as the rent is paid; and in case of ejectment, or in the event of a change of occupancy, whether at the wish of the landlord or tenant, it is the sum of money which the new occupier must pay to the old one for the peaceable enjoyment of his holding."

The Ulster custom tended to enhance the belief on the part of the tenant that his interest in his holding was a perpetual one, for it was stated before the Commission[2] that while the price of the tenant-right frequently amounted to £10, £12, £20 or £25 per acre, and sometimes rose as high as forty years' purchase, the price was not much affected by the tenure on which the land was held, the practice extending to the sale of farms held even from year to year. The right of sale existed

[1] "The Land Question," F. Seebohm, *Fortnightly Review*, 1869, the first definition quoted is that of Lord Dufferin before Mr Maguire's Committee, 1864,—the second that of Mr J. Hancock given before the Landlord and Tenant Commissioners 1844.

[2] See *Digest of Evidence before Devon Commission*, pp. 290, 291.

independent of any improvements having been made by the tenant, and in practice it appeared that it was rarely exercised by an improving tenant, whilst one who had deteriorated his holding was not by that fact precluded from selling. The custom affected more than the rights of possession and sale, it restrained the legal power of the landlord to regulate the rent. Its incidents are well summarised by Mr Justice Field[1] as follows[2] :—

1. "Free sale, subject however to the landlord's right (a) to reject a purchaser upon reasonable grounds, (b) to be paid all arrears of rent due from the seller, (c) to limit the price, that it may not encroach on the value of the landlord's interest.

2. A right of continuous and undisturbed occupancy so long as the rent is paid, subject however to the landlord's right of terminating this occupancy by paying the tenant the market value of his tenant-right.

3. The right to hold at a fair rent, lower than a competition or commercial rent[3]."

The exact origin of this tenant-right is not clearly traceable, but it had its inception in the plantation of James the First, arising not so much from the actual form of the grants then made[4], as from a certain sturdy self-assertiveness in the colony imported, aided by the fact that more of the landlords were resident. Evictions were less frequent in Ulster, and a larger number of the small holders being Protestants they were more in touch with the landlords than was the case elsewhere in Ireland. Continuity of tenure by the tenants

---

[1] A Judge of the High Court of Judicature at Fort William, Bengal.

[2] *Landholding and the Relation of Landlord and Tenant*, p. 288.

[3] See post, p. 141.

[4] At the time of the plantation of James the First, much land was allotted to the London Companies and also to the Irish Society. It is not unfrequently alleged that these Companies proved hard landlords, but it seems without foundation, and the view is

disputed, some ascribing the creation of the custom to their laxity. At present throughout Ireland about 584,327 acres of agricultural land are held by trustees for Charities and public companies. An interesting table of the values given for the tenant-right in various holdings during the years 1873 to 1880 is given by Mr Finlay Dun in his *Landlords and Tenants in Ireland*, pp. 130 and 131.

probably established by degrees a customary authority which ultimately extended equally to Protestant and Catholic; for when the repression of Irish manufactures drove large masses of the Protestant holders to emigrate, the Catholics, who took their places, assumed those rights in the soil which user had attached to the Ulster holdings.

These customary rights established sufficient binding force to regulate the dealings of the tenants *inter se*, and also the relations of landlord and tenant, without the assistance of the Legislature, indeed actually in spite of it; while once established they obtained a certain hold upon the minds of the landlords, who in many cases became pronouncedly in their favour. At first sight this is somewhat curious, since the usage trenches deeply on the legal privileges of the landlord[1]; but on examination the reason of the change of sentiment is plain. The landlord's claim for arrears was a first charge upon the sum obtained by the outgoing tenant, and the rent reserved, if lower than a competitive rent, yet possessed a greater degree of certainty. The power of refusing consent to the introduction of a new tenant upon reasonable grounds, also influenced the landlord in favour of the custom; as did the fact of his having a voice in the regulation of the price paid for the tenant-right, which enabled him to prevent the holding being taken at a cost likely to cripple the new tenant, and to make him an unsatisfactory substitute, unable to improve the holding or to pay rent. There were, however, unsatisfactory features in the custom. The interest for which the incoming tenant might have paid as much as twenty years' purchase was not in reality a stable one, but was legally at the will of the landlord. Even if the strength of the usage granted a certain security of tenure the custom did not itself attempt to define what was to be held a fair rent—obviously a matter of opinion—nor did it itself provide for the increase of rent natural on any advance in the value of the land[2]. These uncertainties in the custom led to a slight

---

[1] The Devon Commissioners held that the tenant-right was an undue interference with the rights of the landlords, see *Digest*, p. 290.

[2] "No principles for the calculation of this fair rent were ever so generally received as to become part of the custom. It was conceded that the land-

amount of friction even in Ulster, though the position there was removed wide as the poles from the universal bad feeling and thinly veiled revolt of the rest of Ireland; where though tenant-right existed locally, bearing certain similarities to the northern custom, it was very limited in its extent and uncertain in its operation. A feature in the custom which developed a certain soreness of feeling on the part of the tenants was the fact that when the land decreased in value the loss fell upon the tenant-right, which became valueless when there were no purchasers, or when even the small amount realized was claimed by the landlord for arrears accumulated during the bad seasons. When the value of land dropped so rapidly in 1848, relations were nearly as strained in parts of Ulster as in the south.

In 1850 the "Irish Tenant-right League" was founded, aiming at acquiring legal recognition for a universal tenant-interest resembling that which obtained in Ulster. At first the Protestants of the north and the Catholics of the south made common cause; but religious differences soon separated them, and the agitation did not assume any formidable proportions. There are many reasons why the introduction of the Ulster custom throughout Ireland by means of compulsory legislation would not be a success[1]. As has been shown it is not sufficiently elaborated to fit any relation of landlord and tenant where at least the germ of sympathy does not exist; for while favourable to the tenant in times of prosperity, his apparent liability to, and the seeming exemption of the landlord from, loss when land is depreciated in value, strains their relations to one another. In the case of Ulster too the extraneous means of acquiring wealth, independent of the soil, by manufacturing pursuits provides a more or less constant supply of purchasers for the land when it comes into the

lord might raise the rent from time to time, as the general progress of the country and the condition of agricultural profits justified, but it was asserted he had no right to raise it to such an extent as to destroy the tenant-right, or to absorb the profits due to improvements made by the tenant," Field, p. 288.

[1] See post, p. 139, 141, as to effect of recognition of custom by act of Parliament.

market; while in other parts of Ireland the complete dependence of the population upon agriculture, though increasing the demand for land, restricts the possibility of there being the necessary capital for its purchase in times of depression. Hence the tenant-right would either become merely of nominal value, or else the incoming tenant would take the holding burdened by a load of debt accumulated in raising the purchase money of the tenant-right, and so would be in no position either to do justice to the land, or to give much likelihood of being a satisfactory rent-payer[1].

[1] The tenant too frequently plunged into a sea of financial troubles by raising money on his tenant-right. And see Cobden Essay by Rt Hon. M. Longfield.

CHAPTER IX.

FREE TRADE IN LAND.

THE years following 1848 brought many social changes in Ireland, but it is unquestionable that the surface prosperity of the land increased in no ordinary degree. Middlemen had practically disappeared, and absenteeism was greatly diminished. The rise in the prices of agricultural products swelled the wealth of a country where farming was almost the only widely cultivated pursuit; and, despite the fact that the productive land devoted to tillage diminished by 140,000 acres between 1855 and 1868[1], the bank deposits of the peasants increased to very considerable sums[2]. A veil of apparent well-being was drawn over the rents and chasms of the social system, and during these years many thought the Irish question solved. It needed but the touch of adversity, however, to bring out in relief all the discords of the conflicting claims of owner and occupier. The new landlords who had purchased under the Incumbered Estates' Act[3] had certainly improved the productive powers of the land, but the insecurity of the tenant-interest was still an unsolved problem; nay more, the complexity of the cross claims was accentuated, for the business character of their investment in Irish land made the landlords not unnaturally tenacious of their full powers.

In 1860[4] an Act was passed so calculated to re-open every half-healed wound in the union of the two land classes that it is almost a matter of amazement that it should have been expected by many who had studied the subject, to prove

---

[1] Field, p. 291 (Note).
[2] Ibid. p. 292.
[3] 11 & 12 Vict. c. 48. See ante p. 111.
[4] 23 & 24 Vict. c. 154.

the *Deus ex machinâ* of the land question. The principle of the Act was simplicity itself, it was merely free trade in land. That such an idea as that of placing landed relations upon the same basis as mercantile transactions should have commended itself to the speculative purchaser through the Incumbered Estates' Court is natural enough; he desired nothing better than that untrammelled contractual relationships should be regarded as the foundation of his position; it freed him from all obligations, save those of a fair mercantile connection, to his tenants. But that the principle should have commended itself to the uninterested observer is more remarkable. The vital change in the system of land ownership created by this Act has been little appreciated; yet the whole feudal theory of real property crumbled into dust before it, and tenure ceased to exist. By one enactment of the Legislature the reciprocal rights of landlord and tenant[1] were shifted from the basis of status to that of contract.

The number of purchasers under the Incumbered Estates' Act was very large; within eight years of its passing, 3,197 properties were sold, and bought by no less than 7,216 purchasers[2]; the landlord interest exerted in favour of the Act of 1860 would therefore be considerable. The hold that the theories of political economy had gained at this time was probably the explanation of its commending itself to uninterested persons. Free trade was the key to every difficulty. To place landlord and tenant on the equal platform of contractual rights; to enable the landowner to sell or let his land as he could sell or let his horses, and to make the tenant purchase or hire his holding as he might a cart, was looked upon as the plain solution of the whole land question. It was never realized that a rule which may be obvious equity in one society may work wrong in another. It is apparent that to the Irish tenant, who considered that he had vested interests in the soil, the contractual theory would be perfectly incomprehensible. According to the tenant's view if *A* purchased the estate of

---

[1] The very word tenant, though used here, is inapplicable to the rela-   tions established by this Act.

[2] Of whom 314 only were English.

B, he did so subject to all the (*assumed*) rights of B's tenants to the continued possession of their holdings on payment of rent; but under this Act no such theory would hold for a moment. A becomes owner of the estate: at the end of the current year[1] of their tenancy, the mass of holdings are legally terminated; A feels no bond uniting him to the tenants, and though he may continue their possession in their holdings it is on a totally different footing. The relation established between A and C (an old tenant) is in A's estimation simply this— " I (A) have contracted with you (C) to give you quiet possession of a certain holding for a payment of £— for the period of one year." Now C on the other hand imagined the relation established to be a mere continuation of the practically perpetual interest which he considered he had held in the soil when his rent had to be paid to B, changed only in so far that the said rent had now to be paid to A.

There was, however, a more serious objection to the Act of 1860 than the conflicting views of landlord and tenant, an objection which proved destructive to the whole theory on which the Act was based. When contractual relations are established if the respective rights of the contracting parties are to be satisfactorily settled both parties should act with freedom. The binding agreement which is to limit and define their mutual obligations should not be rendered unjust by the compulsion of circumstance operating against one party and not against the other. The demand for land was largely in advance of the supply, its possession being almost an essential of existence to the tenant. Devoid of capital, and unskilled in any art save the rudest cultivation of the soil, the Irish small holder felt himself bound to get the land at any cost. What freedom of contract could under such circumstances exist between the landlord and tenant? The rent to be rendered for the subject-matter of their contract was fixed not by the consent of both parties but by the obligatory acceptance by the tenant of the landlord's terms. A notice to quit did not convey to the tenant that he

---

[1] It has been explained before that almost all the holdings were from year to year.

must either make a new agreement with the landlord—should
he think fit—upon different terms, or else take another holding
elsewhere; it said, "you are without capital, there is no land to
be got elsewhere, you must agree to whatever your landlord
proposes, or you must leave a cherished home and be cast without resource upon the world." Freedom of contract was scarcely
possible in such a case as this. The notice to quit was used by
the new landlords in a purely mercantile manner; they assumed
the right given them by statute to sell their goods in the best
market; the notice to quit produced invariably an acceptance
of the higher rental demanded, and they did not consider it
their business to look beneath the surface for causes when the
effect seemed so satisfactory. Having raised by such means
the nominal rent roll of his estate, the speculative purchaser
frequently sold it at the increased value suggested by its
nominal incoming, and the new owner[1] naturally extorted the
full amount of the rents on the strength of which he had
bought the estate.

So sweeping was the change introduced by the Landlord
and Tenant Law Amendment Act (Ireland) 1860[2] that it
merits great attention[3]. By sec. 3 it is enacted that "the
relation of landlord and tenant shall be deemed to be founded
on the express or implied contract of the parties and not upon
tenure or service, and a reversion shall not be necessary to such
relation, which shall be deemed to subsist in all cases in which
there shall be an agreement by one party to hold land from or
under another in consideration of any rent." In so short a
section is swept away all the law of feudal landed relations, and
half a dozen words suffice to extinguish the necessity of a
reversion which was the keystone of the system. The functions of the law, moreover, are changed by this substitution

---

[1] See Richey, p. 59.

[2] 23 & 24 Vict. c. 154.

[3] It was stated by the Bessborough
Commission that this Act of 1860
produced but little effect, but an
examination of the Act will show the
complete revolution made in the
nature of land holding in Ireland

and the remarkable contrast between
the complete negation of tenant-right
in the Act of 1860 and the practical
creation, if not recognition, of it by the
Acts of 1870 & 1881. To the influence
of the Act of 1860 in showing vividly
the difficulties of the land problem
the later Acts are largely due.

of a basis of contract instead of status for the reciprocal rights
of landlord and tenant. The law is no longer employed in
defining the relative positions of the two classes, but merely in
enforcing by its sanctions the agreements made between
them[1]. Another inroad on the old established rules regulating
the rights and liabilities created by a transfer of land is found
in sections 12 and 13[2], the first of which transfers to the
assignee of the landlord the benefit or liability which would
have accrued to the original landlord on his covenants and
agreement, while the latter, in similar manner, allows the
transfer of the benefit and liabilities of the covenants and
agreements of the original tenant to his assignee[3]. Here the
contractual theory is seen in full force; unfettered by the old
rules of covenants which did or did not run with the land, the
assignee either of landlord or tenant merely steps into the shoes
of one of the original parties to the contract.

In one instance an omission in the Act is remarkable. In the
past so great troubles had been caused by the non-recognition of
the right of the tenant to compensation for his permanent improvements, that it is curious that this Act, which so vastly
facilitated the transfer of land, did not deal fully with this
question. The claim of a tenant whose term is closed by the
voluntary action of the landlord to compensation for improvements is even recognised by the Brehon Law. "If the land has
been let for hire, and no time has been specified, whatever
length of time he shall be upon it, whether with necessity or
without necessity he goes, he shall leave behind the erections.
If he be noticed (to quit), whether it is with or without necessity,
he may carry away his erections with him. If a term has been
specified for him, and the term has expired, he shall leave his
erections (behind)[4]." It is of course plain that under the contractual theory a tenant would have no inherent right to claim

---

[1] *Irish Land Laws*, A. G. Richey,
p. 8.
[2] These sections together with sec.
14, repealed 11 Anne c. 2, s. 6.
[3] But the original tenant was not
discharged from his liability unless he

had given notice in writing to the
landlord of the particulars of the
assignment.
[4] *Ancient laws of Ireland*, Vol. IV.,
pp. 132 and 183, quoted by Richey.

for his improvements at the termination of his contract as they were voluntary, he being only required by his agreement to leave the land as he got it. It is to be regretted, therefore, that an attempt was not made to set the vexed subject at rest by specific enactment. The absence of any provision for this purpose is the more noticeable as the law of removable fixtures[1] received an important extension by the Act of 1860, by which not only were trade and agricultural fixtures allowed to be taken by the tenant (as under the Act of 1851[2]), when erected with consent and removed during the tenancy, but in addition permission was given to remove them after the termination of the holding, and although they had been erected without leave. This privilege was given by section 17, which allowed "personal chattels, engines, and machinery, and buildings accessorial thereto, erected and affixed to the freehold by the tenant at his sole expense, for any purposes of trade, manufacture, or agriculture, or for ornament, or for the domestic convenience of the tenant in his occupation of the demised premises, and so attached to the freehold that they can be removed without substantial damage to the freehold or to the fixture itself" to be removed, provided that they had not been erected under any obligation or contrary to any agreement. Such removal to be effected by the tenant, or his executors or administrators either (1) during the tenancy, or (2) within two calendar months after its determination[3] (when the tenancy determines by some uncertain event, and without the act or default of the tenant). This provision certainly bettered the position of the tenant as regards movable fixtures, but no effort was made to deal with the question of permanent improvements. The dwelling, such as it was, on the holding had almost always been erected either by the tenant or some ancestor of his, but no compensation could be obtained for it; and the fact that in general all the permanent improvements were, unlike the

---

[1] Dr Richey pointed out that much of the rigid and inequitable character of the English law on this subject was caused by the incomplete manner in which Bracton adopted the rules of the Roman law. See Bracton, l. 1, c. 1, s. 4, and Richey, p. 45.

[2] 14 & 15 Vict. c. 25, s. 3.

[3] Unless it is otherwise provided by the contract of tenancy.

English custom, provided by the tenant, made a rule which worked fairly in England, burdensome in Ireland.

Before leaving this subject it should be noticed that by another Act of 1860 called the Tenure and Improvement of Land (Ireland) Act[1] a hesitating attempt had been made to deal with the question. The third part of this Act, which treats of improvements made by agricultural tenants in their holdings, provides for their compensation for those of a certain class (such as reclaiming land or erecting farm buildings) by an annuity charged on the lands in which they have been made[2], the labour of the tenant to be reckoned in the compensation[3]. The right of compensation thus given, however, was only exercisable when the improvements had been made with the consent of the landlord[4], and when they could not have been exacted by the owner in pursuance of any contract or custom[5]. The Act, though doubtless a step in the right direction, did not touch the heart of the difficulty, as it merely affected prospective improvements[6].

Returning to the consideration of 23 & 24 Vict. c. 154, it is plain, that being based on the contractual theory, it would differ in its way of viewing the subject-matter of the contract from the English Common Law rule. Accordingly section 40 enacted that if any dwelling-house or other building constituting the substantial matter of the demise, was held by the tenant without an express covenant by him to repair, and was destroyed, became ruinous and uninhabitable, or incapable of beneficial occupation or enjoyment without fault of the tenant, he had a right to determine the tenancy by surrender. The English Common Law rule in such a case, despite the destruction of the subject of the lease, would have held the tenant liable for the rent during the term.

---

[1] 23 & 24 Vict. c. 153.

[2] *Ibid.* sec. 36, and any other lands lying adjacent to such, and held of the same owner under the same demise.

[3] *Ibid.* sec. 44.

[4] *Ibid.* sec. 39 and 40.

[5] Sec. 36. This Act did not seek to interfere with any established customs as to compensation &c., see sec. 62.

[6] A defence of the limited character of this measure, and a good sketch of its general character, will be found in the speech made by Mr Cardwell when introducing the Bill. See Hansard's 3rd series, vol. CLVII. p. 1553—1566.

It has been seen [1] that the process of distress as a means of obtaining rent had declined. The Act of 1860 of course swept away the whole theory on which the right of feudal distress was built up, namely, the entry of the lord to compel performance of the feudal services. It did not, however, abolish this remedy for non-payment, but by section 51 [2] limited its action to the recovery of one year's rent. The effect of this section was to throw into more than usual prominence the remedy of ejectment, which had for some time been gradually more and more resorted to by the landlords. When the much-abused right of ejectment is first met with in the history of Irish land law its exercise was limited to cases where there was (1) a lease, and (2) such lease contained a proviso for re-entry. In 1731 [3] the power was extended to those cases in which there was some lease, minute, or contract in writing, provided a whole year's rent or more was in arrear, though there was no actual clause of re-entry. An Act of the present reign [4] further extended the right to bring an ejectment to the case of tenancies where no written agreement existed, provided the annual rent of the holding was under £50 and a year's rent in arrear. Finally, the Act of 1860 [5] allowed ejectments when a year's rent was in arrear [6] although the tenancy was only implied without a written agreement, and whatever the annual rent: while all the cumbrous legal restrictions as to who had a right to take proceedings against the tenant, which had sprung

---

[1] *Ante*, page 99.

[2] "From and after the commencement of this Act it shall not be lawful for any landlord, or anyone on his behalf, to take or seize any distress for rent which became due more than one year before the making of such distress." 23 & 24 Vict. c. 154, sec. 51.

[3] By 5 Geo. II. c. 4 s. 1 (Irish), and again (in 1751) by 25 Geo. II. c. 13, sec. 2 (Irish), which extended the power to cases where there was an article, minute, or contract in writing without either (1) an actual demise, or (2) a clause of re-entry.

[4] 14 & 15 Vict. c. 57, sec. 73, Civil Bills (Ireland) Act.

[5] 23 & 24 Vict. c. 154, sec. 52.

[6] When rent was less than £100, proceedings might be taken in County Court, see sec. 52 (23 & 24 Vict. c. 154), and Richey p. 54. Two other Acts bearing on ejectment are, one passed in the reign of Anne, and the Eviction Act, 1816 (56 Geo. III. c. 88), providing the remedy by civil bill process—a very important change in the law, as it greatly simplified and cheapened the proceedings. It must be remembered that this Act was passed when the power of the landlords was at its height. See *ante*, p. 106.

up from the rules of the right to rent running with the reversion, were abolished[1], section 53 enacting that, "in any ejectment under this Act it shall not be necessary to allege or prove the making of any demand or re-entry, or the existence of any clause or condition of re-entry in the lease or other contract, or of any legal reversion expectant on the determination of the same, and subsisting in the landlord, provided a tenancy between the parties shall appear to exist, whether by original contract, or by lawful assignment, devise, bequest, or act and operation of law[2]."

The advocates of free trade believed that in 1860 an absolutely fair land system had been established in Ireland; but the Act, though theoretically perfectly just, being founded on pure contract, was unsuited to the state of society to which it was applied. From the very nature of the social system in Ireland free contract could not exist, and after a short time, despite the surface prosperity of the country, signs of disturbance began to appear. Notices to quit began to be largely served on the tenants, and where they escaped eviction it was only by consenting to a higher rate of rent. A large number of evictions of small holders took place in order to enable the landlords to consolidate their estates into larger farms, and between 1861 and 1880 there was a decline of no less than 809,312 in the number of acres under crops, amounting to more than one-seventh of the total acreage under tillage in 1861[3]. The notices to quit, even where no extreme measures were taken, produced an unfortunate result; they marked to the mind of the tenant the uncertainty of his holding, and so were a perpetual cause at once of alarm and anger[4]. An increase in the tenant agitations began to show, and, although it was not openly admitted, those in authority began to perceive that

---

[1] See *The Irish Land Laws*, A. G. Richey, pp. 41—44.

[2] See *post*, p. 180, as to changes in the law of eviction under Act of 1887.

[3] These figures are important, as in Ireland there is always a direct relation between the enlargement of farms and the increase of pasture lands.

[4] In the majority of cases, however, the relations of landlord and tenant were not substantially altered. The worst effects of the Act lay in the way in which it unsettled all existing arrangements and thus aggravated the class feeling in the country.

the Act of 1860 had been a failure, indeed had gone further than that, and proved a new disturbing element.

The principle of the Act was of course just; pure contractual rights with regard to a commodity must of necessity be fair if both parties act freely. In the case of Irish land, however, not only was freedom of contract absent, but also, while the Act of 1860 adopted the theory that the landlord as absolute owner offered for sale or hire a commodity in which the occupier had no vested interest, the tenant held that the land was at least in part his property, and believed in the existence of such interest on the ground (1) of his improvements, and (2) of the assumed practical perpetuity of his tenure. It is evident that here a system of contract, suitable only to an advanced and equably constituted society, and even then suitable only to dealings in a commodity which is amenable to the fair laws of demand and supply, was planted upon a community the social organization of which combined every element of disorder and disintegration. Moreover, the system of contract applied was one of strict mercantile relations, and untempered by concurrent equities. The late Dr Richey, who instituted a comparison at some length between the contractual theory applied to the Irish land law and the theories of the French civilians, as shown chiefly by Pothier's " Traité du Contrat de Bail à Rente" and the French Code, showed very clearly how the mercantile aspect of contract adopted by the Act of 1860 affected the relation of landlord and tenant. Dealing with the manner in which the Civil Law treats the relation of landlord and tenant, which it also bases upon the theory that tenancy is a species of hiring, he pointed out that the difference noticeable between it and the English law was caused by the divergent views which the Roman and English lawyers held as to the original nature of the contract itself, namely:—"(1) The former considered a letting of land for a term to be a quasi-sale, with an equitable warranty that the land was worth the annual rent; the latter that it was a mercantile transaction subject to the rule of ' *caveat emptor*.' (2) The former considered the rent as the owner's share in the proceeds of the farm, and therefore gave to the landlord the right of hypothec, and compelled him to share in the loss occasioned by a deficient harvest; the latter held the rent as something collateral to the letting—cotemporary but not conditional: the tenant made his bargain, and, as in every other mercantile transaction, ran the chance of gain or loss. (3) The former considered the several agreements of the tenant, whether expressed or implied, as conditions precedent of his possession, and held, therefore, that the landlord could bring his action to re-enter upon the breach of any agreement, expressed or implied; the latter, considering all such agreements (except that for the payment of rent) as collateral, gave the landlord no right to re-enter, and left him to his personal action for damages in all except the one excepted case[1]."

That the basis of mercantile contract was unsuited to the case of the Irish land system is clear, but when the fact was at length realized it was found necessary to proceed with the utmost caution with regard to remedial measures. It might be obvious to those who looked beneath the surface that the creation of pure contractual relations, unfettered by equitable obligations, had been a grave error, but enormous interests were concerned under the change which had been adopted. The purchasers under the Incumbered Estates' Act 1848, and the Landed Estates' Act 1858, had always expected freedom of transfer to be attached to their purchases; the Act of 1860 seemed to them the essence of justice, and it was impossible to blink the fact that they had invested their money on the strength of a State guarantee. Again, had it been openly declared that the principle of the Act of 1860 was wrong, the champions of free trade would at once have cried down so heterodox a notion; for though it was clear that the Act was not working well, it was far from being recognized by the majority of people that rules of abstract fairness may operate oppressively in particular circumstances. When the need for new legislation therefore became imperative, the framers of the Act of 1870 approached the subject with great caution.

[1] *The Irish Land Laws,* pp. 55, 56.

CHAPTER X.

The Act of 1870.

The Act of 1860 failed, and agrarian outrages followed the feeling of insecurity of tenure which had been fostered. The general situation also was but little affected by the disestablishment and disendowment of the Irish Church by 32 & 33 Vict. c. 42, though it is impossible to pass over this Act, as in one very important feature it proved efficacious in dealing with the land. Its provisions as to sales by the Church Commissioners[1], unlike the clauses of the Acts of 1870 and 1881 dealing with purchase, proved largely successful[2]. This was the more remarkable, since although the amount which might be advanced by the Commissioners—or rather might be credited by them to the purchaser on mortgage—exceeded that which the Land Commissioners were empowered by the Act of 1870 to advance, still the rate of interest to be charged (4 per cent.) was practically higher[3].

In 1870 it was universally admitted that further legislation was a necessity; and on the 15th of February Mr Gladstone moved for leave to bring in a Bill to amend the

[1] Occupying tenants were protected by a right of pre-emption being given to the tenant. See sec. 34, sub-s. (1) and (5):

"The ordinary tenants of the Church numbered 8432, and of these up to November 1st, 1880, 6057 had become owners of their holdings at an average price of 22⅔ years' purchase." *Two Centuries of Irish History*, article by G. Macdonell. The powers of the Commissioners were transferred in 1881 to the Irish Land Commission.

[2] The full amount of purchase-money being £1,674,000. The comparative number of purchasers under this Act and under the Acts of 1870, 1881, and 1885 will be given when dealing with Lord Ashbourne's Act. See *post*, p. 176.

[3] See *post*, p. 153, note, and Report of Bessborough Commission, sec. 87.

law relating to the occupation and ownership of land in Ireland as regarded agricultural[1] or pastoral holdings. He admitted that it was but a tardy measure; that, following as it did in many ways the lines suggested by the Report of the Devon Commission, its efficacy would have been probably greater, and its action certainly more beneficial, had it been introduced some twenty years before[2]; and then in a speech of much power urged the acceptance of a Bill drawn upon similar lines to, but in bolder fashion than, the Commissioners' report[3]. The objects aimed at were threefold, (1) to give some security of tenure to the tenant by making it a matter of expense and trouble for the landlord to exact his full legal rights; (2) to settle the question of improvements by acknowledging the tenant's claim to compensation; and (3) to facilitate the establishment of peasant owners by means of certain provisions for purchase known as the 'Bright Clauses.'

It is apparent at once that the legislation of this Act is in a manner retrograde, for by the Act of 1860 absolute free trade in land had been established, while the restrictions now suggested were a limitation of the right of free contract, and amounted to a creation on the part of the Legislature of a tenant-

[1] The provisions for compensation did not touch demesne lands, holdings in virtue of being a hired labourer, lettings in conacre, or holdings stated in writing to be for a temporary purpose, or cottage allotments not exceeding a quarter of an acre (33 & 34 Vict. c. 46, sec. 15), and the Act only applied to holdings agricultural or pastoral (sec. 71).

[2] See Hansard, 3rd series, vol. cxcix. p. 334. "Had these recommendations (i. e. those of the Devon Commissioners) been acted upon at the time, it is probable that at this moment no Irish land question would be before the House for discussion."—Mr Gladstone.

[3] Various figures were quoted by Mr Gladstone to show the need of further legislation. Alluding to the increase of pasture lands as a source of loss to the lower classes he said, "Between 1860 and 1868 the pasturage of Ireland has increased by about 560,000 acres, and the tillage of Ireland has decreased during that period about 400,000 acres. We are given to understand that, inasmuch as meadow land is reckoned under land in tillage, and has considerably increased, the real decrease of tillage land is greater still." Again, dealing with the Poor Law statistics he stated that down to 1860 there had been a decrease in the pressure on the poor rates, and "in that year the number of persons seeking relief, who in 1849 might have been counted, so to speak, by millions, was 170,000; but in 1868 the number had increased to 289,000." See Hansard, 3rd series, vol. cxcix, pp. 341, 342.

interest in the land. The claims of the tenants are, it is true, never definitely stated throughout the Act, nor indeed would it have been easily possible for the Government to fully state them. The English belief in the absolute character of freehold ownership had never permitted an open acknowledgement of a right, on the part of the Irish tenant from year to year, to any possessory interest in his holding save the yearly tenancy. While in addition since 1860 the absolute property in the land, subject only to existing tenancies, had been recognized as residing in the landlords.

The purchasers in the Incumbered Estates' Court of lands held by tenants from year to year had been formally released by the Act of 1860 from any obligation to their tenantry (after the termination of the year current at the time of their purchase), other than resulted from a contractual letting and hiring. Neverthless, although it was effected merely in a negative manner, further rights of the tenants in the soil were clearly recognized in 1870. The principle of the Act, by which security of tenure was intended to be conferred, was that of making the landlord pay a compensation for disturbance to the tenant against whom he thought fit to exercise his undeniable legal right of eviction. Since, therefore, the landlord was unable to exercise his rights without compensating the tenant, it is evident that the latter practically acquired an interest in the land equal in value to the amount of such compensation[1]. The tenant in fact had his rights increased to the same extent that the landlord's powers were diminished.

The right of the tenant to compensation for disturbance, however, did not exist if he held for a term certain exceeding 31 years; and ejectments for non-payment of rent, or for breach of any conditions against assignment, subletting, bankruptcy, or insolvency were not deemed disturbances within the meaning of the Act[2]. The cause of the 31 years' limit was an endeavour to stimulate the granting of leases for this length of

---

[1] Dr Richey well pointed out that whereas it was urged that this provision merely compelled bad landlords to act like good ones, its real effect was to make eviction a privilege of the wealthy. *Irish Land Laws*, p. 64.

[2] 33 & 34 Vict. c. 46, s. 9.

time; and the compensation allowed for disturbance in other
cases was based on the theory that it was the voluntary act of
the landlord, for which damages were due to the tenant, who
had not by his conduct conduced to such termination. Now,
granting for the moment that such a compensation was equitable in the case of tenants from year to year, it is hard to see
upon what possible grounds it could be supported in the case
of a tenancy for a term certain less than 31 years which determined by effluxion of time. It cannot be urged that this is in
any sense determination by the act of the landlord, and why
then should he be liable to compensate the tenant ?

As a general fault in the whole Act it must be urged that
its intricacy was eminently unsuited to grapple successfully
with a popular evil; its subtlety rendering it unintelligible to
the greater portion of the class who were intended to benefit
by it, and the necessary invocation of a court of justice before
its benefits could be received both conflicting with the pre-
judices of the tenants, and causing expense to bar some claims.
There are other and more serious objections, however, which
it is well to glance at before the Act is examined in detail.
Chief amongst these stands the fact that it did not openly
touch the root of the peasants' grievance, money for his improvements doubtless seemed to him a boon, and compensation
for disturbance was good in his eyes, but it was for neither of
these things that he was striving ; what he desired was to be
able always to stay in his holding. Compensation was a plea-
sant idea certainly, but then it was only gained when all he
desired was lost, namely, when he was forced from his home.
Moreover, when he had the money it was wonderfully useless
to him ; for as was pointed out by the late Dr Richey[1] he knew
but two uses for it, either he must stock a farm (and the
number of farms was limited while the demand was excessive),
or he must place it in a bank on deposit receipt. Again the
compensation, the payment of which was to deter the landlord
from an arbitrary exercise of his powers, was frequently advanced by the incoming tenant[2], necessity driving the tenants

[1] p. 94.   [2] Richey, p. 96.

to overwhelm one another in their frantic struggles to obtain the possession of land. Further, the idea that leases for 31 years would prove to be objects of desire to the tenants was not justified in the event; and for this there were two principal reasons : (1) the tenant from year to year regarded his holding as a species of perpetuity[1] (and the effect of the Act of 1870 was certainly to strengthen him in this impression) therefore he regarded a lease for a term certain as constituting a waiver by him of his rights in the soil and an unjust limitation of them : (2) on the termination of a tenancy for more than 31 years no claim could be made by the tenant for compensation for disturbance, whereas such a right was given by the Act of 1870 in the case of a yearly tenancy if determined by the act of the landlord.

In addition to these faults in the Act it should be noticed that it contained no provision regulating in any way the rate of fair rent, and even when it recognised the existence of, and for the first time gave the formal sanction of the Legislature to the Ulster custom, it took no steps to remedy its weak point of uncertainty as to what constituted a fair rent. The result of the Act was in no way what had been so confidently hoped and expected; its general tendency indeed proved merely to be to increase the amount of rent asked for the peasant holdings[2]. Nevertheless, though it proved abortive, as far as the final solution of the Irish land troubles were concerned, it is a most ingenious fabric, and while an examination in detail brings out many unexpected flaws in its construction, it will always remain a most important landmark in the history of Irish law. It is a remarkable example of the dexterous handling which Mr Gladstone so invariably applies to his legislative creations. Unfortunately it proved rather the fruitful mother of other troubles than the final settlement of the question dealt with.

The Act of 1870[3], after having been vigorously opposed in

---

[1] " It is not the right of the rent-receiver, but the right of the cultivator, with whom the idea of property is connected in the Irish mind." *England and Ireland*, J. S. Mill.

[2] See § 19 Report of Bessborough

Committee.

[3] 33 & 34 Vict. c. 46, entitled " An Act to amend the law relating to the occupation and ownership of land in Ireland."

Committee in both Houses of Parliament, became law on the 1st of August of that year[1], and has been rightly described as one of the most remarkable and original pieces of legislation in the Statute Book. It is divided into five parts, dealing respectively with (1) the law of compensation to tenants[2], (2) the sale of land to tenants[3], (3) advances by, and powers of, the Board of Works[4], (4) and (5) supplemental and miscellaneous provisions[5]. Taking the most important clauses in detail, the first section of the Act deals with the question of the Ulster tenant-right. No alteration or limitation is suggested, it is simply enacted that the custom shall receive the sanction of law, and be capable of regular legal enforcement when proved to exist. It has already been pointed out[6] that this Ulster custom, though widely preferable to entire insecurity of tenure, was deficient through its lack of sufficiently defining incidents of the custom, such as fair rent, which were nevertheless essential to its existence. The recognition by Legislature of the custom enhanced these weak points. The usual plan of employing local valuators to estimate the worth of the holding for the purpose of fixing the fair rent, when a readjustment was necessary, was unsuitable to a legalized system, and the action of the Courts failed to uphold the most useful feature of the usage, viz. continuity of tenure. In short, the action of the Courts when applied to the Ulster customs deprived them at once of the flexibility to circumstance which was their chief boon.

The Ulster customs differed entirely from 'customs of the country' in the sense in which it is usual to employ the words as indicating a usage which must have been deemed to have been in the contemplation of both parties when they made their contract, and which hence can rightly be held an implied term thereof. As was pointed out by the late Dr Richey, such a custom as that by which a tenant was entitled to a way-going crop, etc., is one which a landlord, when creating a yearly tenancy, may be held to have contemplated; "but a

[1] About a fortnight after the breaking out of the Franco-German war.
[2] Secs. 1 to 31.
[3] Secs. 32 to 41.
[4] Secs. 42 to 56.
[5] Pt. 4, secs. 57 to 64 ; pt. 5, secs. 65 to 73.
[6] *Ante*, p. 121, 122.

custom, such as that of Ulster, to pay to the tenant the value of
his occupancy upon the legal determination of his tenancy, was
one contradictory to the nature of the estate created, and excluded
by the terms of the contract itself"[1]. It was therefore unjust to
have expected the formal recognition of the custom from the
Irish Courts before 1870, and its working in the form perforce
assumed under the Act, both deprived it of many of its inherent advantages, and also showed that legal forms did not
suit the usage. What was really required by the tenant under
the Ulster custom, who applied to the Court for help on account
of receiving from his landlord a notice to pay higher rent or quit
his holding, was not a judgment against the landlord for the
amount of his tenant-right, but a decree for the specific performance of the customary compact of continued holding at a
fair rent[2]. The Court, however, did not deal with the settlement
of fair rents, and the tenant's demand took the form of a claim
for compensation[3], with the result that neither landlord nor
tenant in all probability got what they required. The landlord
was first compelled to pay a considerable sum, and then had the
land thrown upon his hands, when all he desired was to raise
the rent of the holding, possibly on account of an increase in
the value of the land; and the tenant was presented with a
sum of money which he did not want, and for which he had little
use, while he was deprived of the holding to which he was
so deeply attached. Nor did the Act prevent the raising of
rent, for if the landlord, when the tenant-right was in the
market, stated that in future the rent would be increased, this
did not usually deter the purchaser, and the loss of value in the
tenant-right fell upon the outgoing tenant who received a less
sum for the goodwill of his holding[4].

The exact position taken by the Act of 1870 with regard
to the Ulster customs was not in any way to render them obligatory on the tenant should he choose to waive them and claim
under the general rights given, but merely to offer a legal

[1] *Irish Land Laws*, p. 102. Dr
Richey refers in support of this view
to the exhaustive judgment in Ramsden
v. Dyson, L. R. 1. *H. of L.* 129.

[2] See Report of Bessborough Committee, 17, 18.

[3] See Field, p. 312.

[4] *Ibid.* p. 314.

sanction for their incidents if the tenant chose to demand it and could prove the custom. The usage might, and generally did, vary in different parts of Ulster (indeed even contiguous estates might differ in minor points), but the tenant was merely required to prove the particular customs, and that they had prevailed for a reasonable time, and had not been created in contemplation of the Act[1].

Leaving the subject of holdings regulated by custom, the Act then proceeds to lay down the rules under which compensation for disturbance in the absence of usage is to be computed. As has been said, the whole principle involved in allowing such a claim, which was tantamount to the vesting of a right in the land in the tenant, independent of his contract with the landlord, was foreign to the theory of the Act of 1860. The use of the term 'compensation for disturbance' also was singularly unfortunate, as, even if it applied to the case of a yearly tenancy, it is absolutely contrary to common sense when applied to the claim against the landlord of a tenant who held for a term certain which ended by completion of the term[2].

When Mr Gladstone described the nature of the compensation clauses in the Act[3] he prefaced his remarks by giving a comparison of the rent returns of the past century in Ireland, England and Scotland, showing that while in the first case they had only about doubled, in England they had trebled, and in Scotland sextupled. He argued, therefore, as a proof of the advantages of security of tenure to the tenant, that the rents had increased in the three countries in the direct ratio of the security of the tenure of the cultivator[4]. He then carried the same argument further by shewing that the increase in Ulster had been larger than in the rest of Ireland owing to the increased rights of the tenant under the Ulster custom, and the consequent restriction of the powers of the landlord[5]. The form which compensation for disturbance

[1] See Kevan v. Lord de Ros, quoted by Richey, p. 106.

[2] See *ante*, p. 138, and Richey, p. 66 (note).

[3] When moving for leave to bring in the Bill, February 15th, 1870.

[4] See Hansard, 3rd series, Vol. cxcix. p. 355, 356.

[5] Mr Gladstone gave the following figures for Ireland — not including

in the absence of custom ultimately assumed when embodied in the Act of 1870[1], presents on analysis the following features:—

A. The tenant is only entitled to compensation under the general clauses when:—

(By section 3,)

1. He is not entitled to claim under the Ulster or similar customs: or

2. Being so entitled elects not to claim under them.

3. Is disturbed by the act of the landlord:—

While for the purposes of the Act the following are not deemed disturbances by the landlord of such a kind as to entitle the tenant to compensation :—

(By section 9,)

(1) An ejectment for non-payment of rent.

(2) An ejectment for breach of any conditions against assignment, subletting, bankruptcy or insolvency.

Provided that the Court may, if it think fit, hold an ejectment for non-payment of rent to be a disturbance in the case of a tenancy existing at the time of the passing of the Act, and continuing to exist without alteration of rent up to the time of such determination, if

a. rent arrears did not accrue within the last three years, and if any earlier arrears remained due from the tenant at the time of commencing the ejectment:—or

b. the rent of the holding is under £15 per annum and the Court certifies that the rent is exorbitant[2].

Ulster : Rentals in 1779 (according to Arthur Young), £5,000,000, in 1869 £9,200,000, i.e. less than double. While in Ulster during the same period the increase was more than threefold, though the soil was far less productive. See Hansard, 3rd series, Vol. cxcix. p. 357.

[1] 33 & 34 Vict. c. 46.

[2] This provision turned out almost inoperative, and was for the most part unnoticed, the use of the word ' exorbitant ' contributing to this result. Bessborough Commission, § 21.

(By section 10,)

    (3)   The resumption by the landlord from a yearly tenant of not more than $\frac{1}{25}$th of his holding for the purpose of erecting labourers' cottages thereon, and which was resumed after six months' notice to the tenant, unless the Court shall hold such resumption unreasonable.

(By section 14,)

    (4)   Where the yearly tenant is evicted for the persistent exercise of any right

        a. not necesssary to the due cultivation of his holding :—and

        b. forbidden by his agreement with his landlord.

    (5)   Where the yearly tenant is evicted for persistently and unreasonably refusing to allow the landlord, or those authorized by him, to enter on the holding for certain specified purposes, e.g. mining, cutting turf, &c.

B.   The landlord can deduct from the compensation :--

(By section 3,)

    1.   Amount of arrears of rent due by the tenant or his predecessors in title.

    2.   Sums due in respect of deterioration of the holding owing to the non-observance on the part of the tenant of any covenant.

    3.   Any taxes due on the holding and payable by the tenant.

C.   The tenant is not entitled to compensation who, after the passing of the Act :—

(By section 3,)

    1.   Subdivides or sublets his holding without the consent in writing of the landlord.

    2.   After prohibition in writing lets it in conacre, save for the purpose of being solely used for green crops.

    3.   Holds for a lease for more than 31 years.

(By section 12,)

    4.   Has contracted in writing not to make such claim.

Provided that

(1) his holding is over £50 annual value,

(2) it is not subject to customary usage.

(By section 13,)

5.   When the tenancy is from year to year existing at the time of the passing of the Act assigns

(1) without the consent of the landlord, and

(2) landlord does not accept assignee.

Provided that

    I. sufficient rent is in arrears at the time of the assignment to render the tenant liable to eviction :—or

    II. such assignment is contrary to the customary usage of the estate :—or

    III. the Court thinks the landlord's refusal to accept the new tenant to be reasonable[1].

On examination it is seen that one of the most striking of the above provisions is that which enables an ejectment by the landlord, even for non-payment of rent or for breach of covenant, to be held a disturbance (and hence to entitle the tenant to compensation), *if the holding is under £15 annual value*[2] *and the Court certifies that the rent is exorbitant.* The reason of the exemption of the two cases of non-payment of rent and breach of covenant from the disturbances by the landlord which were penalized in damages is the fact that the eviction results from the tenant's own act. It is hard to logically support the exemption of holdings under £15 from this rule on account of the rent being exorbitant, as such an argument would apply equally to holdings at a higher rental. The reason for the enactment no doubt was a desire to shelter the small tenants whose rent was forced up by the action of the landlord, who might hence be said to be himself the origin of the act on which eviction was taken. Plainly however, when the high rent was the result of the 'reckless

---

[1] The transmission of a tenancy by bequest to certain near relations or its devolution by operation of law is not such an assignment as would justify the landlord in refusing compensation. Sec. 13.

[2] See *ante*, p. 143.

competition' of the *tenants* an exemption cannot be supported on logical grounds, as the termination of the tenancy by eviction on non-payment of rent in a double sense originates with the tenant, in that (1) he did not pay his rent, and (2) he voluntarily undertook more than he could perform[1]. Passing from the grounds on which the compensation was to be given, or on which exemption could be claimed by the landlord, to the nature and amount of the compensation itself, the rules of the Act of 1870 appear open to objection. Section 3 enacts that the limit of the compensation is to be regulated thus; holdings valued under the Acts relating to the valuation of rateable property in Ireland at an annual value of

(1) £10 and under, a sum which shall in no case exceed seven years' rent.

(2) Above £10 and not exceeding £30, a sum which shall in no case exceed five years' rent.

(3) Above £30 and not exceeding £40, a sum which shall in no case exceed four years' rent.

(4) Above £40 and not exceeding £50, a sum which shall in no case exceed three years' rent.

(5) Above £60 and not exceeding £100, a sum which shall in no case exceed two years' rent.

(6) Above £100, a sum which shall in no case exceed one year's rent.

But in no case shall the compensation exceed the sum of £250[2].

The late Dr Richey, in criticising the scheme of compensation adopted here, said,—"as the maximum of the compensation in each case is calculated upon the basis, not of the valuation, but of the rent, the amount of compensation varies in the inverse ratio of the value of the interest, which has been lost by the tenant. The higher the rent reserved upon a lease, the less it will fetch at an auction; and on the other hand its

---

[1] See Richey, pp. 73, 74 and note.

[2] 33 & 34 Vict. c. 46, sec. 3. The scale of compensation quoted applies to tenancies created after the passing of the Act, but by the same section compensation for disturbance by the immediate landlord is given on the same scale in the case of yearly tenancies existing at the time of the passing of the Act.

value would be augmented if the rent were reduced. If *A* be
tenant from year to year of a farm valued at £10, and pays a
rent of £15 per annum, and *B* holds a farm of equal rating but
pays only £5 per annum rent, it is manifest that *B*'s interest in
his holding is much more valuable than that of *A* ; under this
section, however, *A* would be entitled to the sum of £105 as
compensation for disturbance, but *B* only to £35[1]."

In addition to the foregoing objections to the system on
which the compensation was calculated[2], it has been already
mentioned that the amount of the compensation to be paid was
found insufficient to check the action of the evicting landlord,
owing to the fact that a new tenant was often to be found who
was ready to pay the compensation to the outgoing tenant in
order to gain possession of the holding. This same fact tended
also to produce large holdings—a most unexpected result—for
if a tenant *A*, who already held a farm on an estate, expressed
a desire to take up other small holdings, and offered to pay the
compensation to the evicted tenants, it is obvious that the
interest of the landlord would be strongly enlisted in the
change. The compensation he would have to pay to *A*, should
he afterwards evict him from the enlarged holding, would
be far less than the combined compensation he would have
had to pay to the other small holders. It is also plain that
the mode of compensation here adopted is a bar to the creation
of improvements by the landlord, since these would, although

---

[1] See Richey, pp. 68 and 69. This
relates of course merely to compensation for disturbance, and is founded
on the theory of the *maximum* value
having been awarded in both cases.
It does not affect the position of *A* and
B as regards compensation for improvements; but it should be noticed
that sec. 3 also enacts that no tenant
of a holding valued at a yearly sum
exceeding £10 and claiming under this
section more than four years' rent, and
no tenant of a holding valued at a
yearly sum not exceeding £10 and
claiming as aforesaid more than five
years' rent, shall be entitled to make

a separate or additional claim for
improvements other than permanent
buildings and reclamation of waste
land.

[2] In practice the result of the statutory limitations of the compensation
for disturbance, combined with the
discretion given to County Court Judges
as to assessal, resulted in a rough and
ready administration of justice. The
Judges taking the tenant as primâ
facie entitled to the full amount of the
compensation, and casting upon the
landlord the onus of proving claims in
reduction.

increasing the rent, at the same time probably raise the compensation which must be paid on terminating the holdings[1].

The difficulty that under compulsion the tenants might agree to contract themselves out of these provisions for compensation was met by section 3, which made such a contract void both in law and equity (subject to exception if the holding was of more than £50 annual value and the contract not to claim was in writing[2]). Mr Gladstone thus justified this enactment: " our desire is to interfere with freedom of contract as little as possible. We are about to interfere with it in regard to the terms on which minor tenancies may be taken up, because we say that in the circumstances of Ireland the tenant is not free ; but as we move upwards in the scale of the value of holdings, at last, undoubtedly, we reach a point where the tenant may be said to be free[3]."

In order to prevent the landlord changing the nature of the tenancies granted, so as to escape on a side issue from his liability to compensation, section 69 enacted that a tenancy at will, or less than a tenancy from year to year, gave the tenant the same rights as to notice to quit and compensation as did a tenancy from year to year. Only one more point need be dealt with before leaving the subject of compensation for disturbance and passing to the enactments as to improvements—this point is the question of the rights of sub-tenants, which is dealt with in section 20 in a highly inadequate manner. By this section, when the estate of the middleman terminates " by reason of disturbance or otherwise" and "involves the interests of any such persons other than the tenant quitting his holding, the Court shall determine the whole amount payable under this Act on the occasion of such tenant quitting his holding and shall direct payment of the same by such person, and to such one or more of the persons interested, and in such manner as the Court thinks just." It is plain that the amount due from the superior landlord to the evicted middleman would probably be a far smaller sum than that to which the combined claims of his tenants would have amounted, had he himself

[1] A very interesting example of this is given by Dr Richey, pp. 70 and 71.   [2] Sec. 12, and see *ante*, p. 145.   [3] Hansard, 3rd series, cxcix. p. 370.

evicted them. Therefore, though the tenant is in each case
turned from his holding, the amount of compensation he receives
is widely different[1]; a very unsatisfactory result[2].

The second object aimed at by the Act of 1870 was the
settlement of the vexed question of improvements by compensating the tenant on the termination of his tenancy for those of
a permanent nature which he had made in his holding. Mr
Gladstone, in his speech on the motion, established very clearly
the equitable claim of the tenants to some such protection.
When alluding to the effect of the Incumbered Estates Act 1848[3],
he drew attention to the fact that while the older class of landlords had but in few cases improperly increased the rents of the
holdings on the ground of improvements which the tenants had
themselves made; yet, when the properties of these landlords
came into the Incumbered Estates Court, "the purchasers
bought them as they were, and no distinction was drawn between
the soil itself and the improvements made by the tenant. So
that the improvements were sold to persons who gave a price for
them; sold away from the tenant to whom they ought to have
belonged; and the price was paid to the outgoing landlord, who
undoubtedly ought not to have been entitled to claim the property in them, and would not have been so entitled if the
legislation recommended in 1845[4] had been adopted[5]".

The form taken by the provisions enacted for the purpose of
thus compensating the tenant was:—that any tenant who is
not entitled (or being entitled does not claim) under the Ulster
or similar customs, may claim compensation for improvements
which have been made by himself or his predecessors in title[6]:
save in the following cases:

---

[1] Dr Richey gives an illustration of
this, pp. 78, 79, and 80.

[2] It should be noticed that by sec. 7
a tenant who has neither claimed compensation for disturbance, nor under a
customary right, is entitled to compensation on leaving his holding for money
paid on coming into his holding by
himself or his predecessors in title with
the express or implied consent of the
landlord; unless (1) the landlord has
given him permission to gain the sum
from the incoming tenant, (2) such
money was paid during the existence
of a lease, before the passing of the
Act.

[3] 11 & 12 Vict. c. 48.

[4] By the Devon Commission.

[5] Hansard, 3rd series, cxcix. p. 344.

[6] 33 & 34 Vict. c. 46, sec. 4.

(1)   When the said improvements have been in existence for 20 years—(unless they consist of permanent buildings or reclamations of waste land,
in which cases he *may* claim).

(2)   When the landlord has prohibited in writing the
making of such improvements as detrimental to
the estate[1].

(3)   When they were made in pursuance of a contract
for valuable consideration.

(4)   When made in contravention of an agreement in
writing not to make such improvements (subject
to the rule as to when such a prohibitory contract is allowed).

(5)   When the landlord has undertaken to make the
said improvements (unless he has failed to do
so within reasonable time).

(6)   When he holds under a lease or written contract
made before the Act in which his right to compensation is expressly excluded.

(7)   When he holds under a lease for 31 years, or one
which has actually so long subsisted:—(but here
compensation is allowed for permanent buildings,
unexhausted manures and reclamation of waste).

(8)   When he is quitting voluntarily, and his landlord has given him permission to dispose of his
interest in the improvements to the incoming
tenant upon such terms as the Court may deem
reasonable, and he has refused or neglected to
avail himself of this permission.

When the amount of compensation is being reckoned all
sums due to the landlord for rent, deterioration of the holding
from breach of the tenant's covenants, or for the tenant's taxes,
may be deducted.

Further regulations in the same section[2] of the Act:—

---

[1] When they appear to the Court to
be detrimental, and are made within
two years after the passing of the Act,
or during the unexpired residue of a
lease granted before the passing of the
Act, sec. 4, sub-s. (1).

[2] 33 & 34 Vict. c. 46, sec. 4.

1. Render void any contract between landlord and tenant whereby the latter is restrained from making improvements required for the suitable occupation of his holding.

2. Render void any contract whereby the tenant is deprived of his right to claim compensation for improvements (save in the cases above excepted; and in holdings over £50 annual value, and not subject to Ulster customs or the like, where the contract is in writing).

3. Enact that when the improvements have been made before the Act, the Court, in considering the amount of the compensation to be granted, shall take into consideration the length of time for which the tenant has had the use of them, or any set-off which may have been granted by the landlord.

While

(By section 6) the landlord or tenant may register their improvements in the Landed Estates Court, and

(By section 5[1]) the presumption of law is stated always to be that any improvements are the work of the *tenant; save in the following cases*, where compensation is claimed for improvements made *before* the Act, and

I. the improvements were made previous to the time when the title accrued by actual sale to the landlord or those through whom he claims.

II. the tenant held under a lease.

III. the improvements were made 20 years before the Act.

IV. the holding is valued at over £100 annual value.

V. the Court holds, on the ground of the practice of the estate, that such ought not to be presumed.

VI. the Court is satisfied that the improvements were not the work of the tenant.

Provided that where it is proved to have been the practice for the landlord to assist in making the improvements the presumption shall be modified accordingly.

The third object aimed at by the Act of 1870 was the

---

[1] Does not apply if (1) holding is subject to Ulster or similar customs; (2) tenant seeks compensation under them.

establishment of peasant proprietors. For this purpose clauses termed the Bright Clauses[1] were inserted in the Act, the intention of which was to facilitate the purchase by a tenant of his holding either

    1. By agreement with his landlord, or

    2. From the Court, in estates directed to be sold by the Landed Estates Court.

In the first case the procedure to be adopted was that when an agreement for the sale had been made between the landlord and tenant, they might jointly (or either of them separately with the assent of the other) apply to the Court to carry out the sale[2].

The powers of purchase given by the Act proved valueless in both the case of a sale by agreement and a forced sale of an incumbered estate[3], but the provisions for sales of the first class proved even more faulty than those regulating the latter. The general faults which marred the Bright Clauses proved to be:—

    (1) The absolute title given by the Landed Estates Court to the purchaser. It seems strange that this power of the Court to give a title which absolutely extinguishes all rights adverse to the terms of the grant should have operated as an evil; for it was not unnaturally supposed that the indefeasible nature of the title given would have constituted its greatest advantage. But the fact that no error could afterwards be remedied, that the title given would hold, even if the clearest rights of third parties proved to have been infringed, or more land than was really saleable had been conveyed, paralyzed the action of the Courts by the nicety of the enquiry needed[4].

---

[1] 33 & 34 Vict. c. 46, sec. 32—41.

[2] 33 & 34 Vict. c. 46, sec. 32.

[3] Mr Justice Field says, "The provisions for facilitating the acquisition by tenants of their holdings forming part of estates the sale of which had been directed by the Landed Estates Court failed chiefly in consequence of the general refusal of the authorities to arrange lots so as to suit the convenience of purchasing tenants, this course being found inconsistent with the interests of owners and incumbrancers." *Landholding*, p. 318.

[4] See Richey, pp. 82 and 85. "A Landed Estates Court conveyance affects not only the rights of the parties to the proceedings, but binds all persons, whether parties or not, and extinguishes all rights which are inconsistent with the terms of the grant by the Court."

(2) The amount which the Commissioners of Public Works in Ireland were allowed to advance to the tenant for the purpose of purchasing his holding was not sufficient. By the Act of 1870[1] the amount was limited to two-thirds of the price of the holding[2], and though it was increased by an Act of 1872[3] to two-thirds of the *value* of the holding (while on being satisfied with the title the Board was able to make advances to tenants purchasing by agreement with the land-lords, without the expense of passing the holding through the Landed Estates Court) it still proved to be inadequate. This was due to two causes :

α. The provision of the Act of 1870[4] that where any such advance was made the tenant was precluded from alienating, assigning, or subletting his holding without the consent of the Board, while any portion of the annuities remained unpaid on pain of forfeiture[5].

β. The Board, considering themselves as trustees for public money, required unexceptionable securities for their advances, and, in the opinion of the tenants, did not act freely in the matter[6].

(3) The difficulty of making the tenants understand their rights under the Act.

The special faults of the Act in regard to sales by agreement were that :—

(1) The landlord is required to deposit with the applica-

---

[1] Sec. 44, 45.

[2] On such an advance the holding was deemed to be charged with an annuity of £5 for every £100 of such advance and so in proportion for any less sum, such annuity to be limited in favour of the Board and to be declared to be repayable in the term of 35 years (33 & 34 Vict. c. 46, s. 44, 45). This makes the rate of interest 3½ per cent. and hence more favourable than the terms of the Church Commissioners, but the proportion to be advanced on mortgage was less, viz. two-thirds in lieu of three-fourths of the purchase-money. See Report of Bessborough Commission, § 87.

[3] 35 & 36 Vict. c. 32, sec. 1.

[4] 33 & 34 Vict. c. 46, sec. 44.

[5] Power was given by the Amending Act of 1872 to commute forfeitures for a sale and to pay the balance of the proceeds to the original purchaser.

[6] See Richey, p. 88. The Board does not seem to have been in any way opposed to the creation of a peasant proprietary.

tion a sum of money as security for costs if required by the Court to do so[1]. In practice, as might have been expected, the result of this was to cast the work of providing this sum upon the tenant.

(2) All the cost of the complicated enquiry which the nature of the title given by the Court rendered necessary (especially heavy when the landlord was only a limited owner) had to be borne by the tenant, and single holdings proved unequal to the task[2].

(3) The estate passed to the tenant, though free from incumbrances, was, by section 36, still liable to certain charges, such as quit rents, rent-charges in lieu of tithes, heriots, charges for draining etc. As pointed out by the late Dr Richey, though these charges were not felt by the tenant paying an annual rent, they were a serious matter to purchasers; since if several tenants purchased their holdings the person entitled to the charge could proceed against any one of them for the amount of the whole charge; and the Court proved slow to use the powers given by section 40[3] to apportion charges, rents and covenants[4]. While in the case of the sale of separate holdings it was not possible to indemnify the purchaser by casting the burden of the charge on the residue of the landlord's estate, as this operation, if frequently repeated, would at length render the residue of his land unsaleable.

The Act of 1870 had to undergo a stormy history. It is probable that the inherent defects of the Act were so great that in any case it would have signally failed to ameliorate the tenants' position even had it had an unchequered career, but

[1] 33 & 34 Vict. c. 46, sec. 34.

[2] This question of excessive costs was dwelt on in the Report of the Committee of the House of Commons 1877–1878.

[3] 33 & 34 Vict. c. 46, sec. 40.

[4] "The Court has always been slow and unwilling to exercise the power of apportioning rent-charges upon the premises sold, and requires it to be clearly shown that the interest of the rent should not in any appreciable degree be made less secure, or less enjoyable, or less marketable. It is idle to suppose that the property of the owner of the head-rent would not be seriously depreciated by being broken into several smaller rent-charges apportioned among the holdings of the tenants who had purchased the fee under the sections in question." Richey, pp. 86, 87.

it was also met by a fatal combination of circumstances. Not only was an agitation, which even if rooted in distress was unscrupulous and fanatical in operation, directed against it; but the very elements conspired to wreck its chances. At first the prosperous seasons veiled the evil, but they only (by raising the credit of the tenants and so enabling them to load themselves with debt) increased the troubles which the subsequent depression brought; and it cannot be denied that the only effect of the Act was to afford new grievances to both landlord and tenant.

CHAPTER XI.

THE ACT OF 1881.

THE years following 1870 were at first years of unusual prosperity for Ireland. In 1872 the exports of goods from Belfast rose to an excess of £2,300,000[1] more than in 1870, and to an excess of £3,400,000 over 1869; though unfortunately this was accompanied by a corresponding increase in the population. The general cotton trade revived, and some remarkable figures are given in Dr Hancock's[2] report of the Irish savings and other banks; he says "the aggregate investments of the Irish people in Government joint-stock banks and savings banks on the 31st of December 1870 were £63,553,251, and on the 31st of December 1871, £67,331,778, showing an increase of £3,778,527, or £6 per cent." In 1875 despite the existence of an element of discontent the relation of landlord and tenant was not unfriendly; and English opinion attached very little importance to the growing Home Rule agitation. In the North of Ireland, however, it was evident that a determined struggle was being made to obtain a larger concession of tenant-right than the Act afforded.

In 1879 a miserable season not only destroyed the potato crop, but also (by the incessant rain preventing the turf from drying) almost caused a fuel famine. The exports of the country diminished, bank deposits sank, and bankruptcies among the tenant farmers became common[3]. The money-lender, that bane of the Irish peasant, pressed for payment, and the agrarian difficulties again became acute. The anti-rent agitation rose

---

[1] See Statement to the Belfast Chamber of Commerce made by Mr Spotten, and quoted in *Annual Register*, 1872.

[2] See *Annual Register*, 1872.

[3] See *Annual Register*, 1879.

in Mayo and Galway, and was carried on in most unscrupulous fashion. Gathering to itself the whole of the disaffected population, and trading on the real misery which the agricultural depression had caused, the movement rapidly became formidable. The Irish Land League was formed, and the agitation was pointedly directed to obtaining for Ireland a peasant proprietorship; the examples of France, Germany and Russia—especially the first—being largely appealed to.

It is very noticeable how far the claims of the tenants were now pushed, and it is in a great measure to this creation of a desire for complete possession of the land that the failure of the Act of 1881 may be ascribed. Had the three F's[1] been given in 1870, when they were practically the limit of the tenants' demand, the settlement of the land question might possibly have been achieved. Unfortunately the Act when passed was only a tardy concession to circumstances, and did nothing to satisfy the wild hopes that had been created. The advocacy of outrage, and the sad catalogue of agrarian crime which the following years present, is a terrible commentary on the force of the passions aroused. The year 1880 was marked by a continued, indeed an increased, depression; the invention of "boycotting" placed a new and most formidable offensive weapon in the hands of the most unscrupulous of the agitators, and the land system of Ireland was practically at a deadlock. In the midst of social tumult and extreme depression Mr Gladstone again essayed the solution of the difficulty.

Fortunately in considering the position of the Irish land system prior to the Act of 1881, we are possessed of two most valuable sources of information in the evidence collected by, and the reports of, two Commissions (called respectively the Richmond and the Bessborough Commissions), appointed to enquire into the agricultural position in Ireland and the working of the Act of 1870. The former of these issued in August 1879, and, though different opinions as to the most advantageous remedies to be applied to the existing evils were held by the Commissioners, the reports and evidence concur in showing:—
(1) That there was widespread distress and dissatisfaction in

---

[1] Fixity of tenure, fair rent, and free sale. See *post*, p. 159, 160.

the country, and (2) That the Act of 1870 had done nothing towards a satisfactory solution of the land question.

The preliminary report issued in January 1881 by the majority of the Commissioners gave us the chief causes of the unfortunate state of landed relations:

1. The inclemency of the seasons, and the failure of the potato crop.

2. Foreign competition.

3. An undue inflation of credit produced by the security afforded by the Land Act of 1870, and by a series of prosperous seasons.

4. The excessive competition for land (mainly due to the fact that apart from the actual possession of the soil, there were few, if any, means of subsistence for the population), which had led to serious abuses, such as:—

   (1)   Unreasonable payments for tenant-right.
   (2)   Arbitrary increase of rents.
   (3)   Overcrowding of the population in certain districts.
   (4)   Minute subdivision of farms[1].

Only one of these heads requires a special mention, that is the one dwelling on the evils of the inflation of credit produced by the Act of 1870. It has been pointed out that, although the object was attained by enactments of a negative kind[2], this Act vested a tangible interest in the land in the tenant. An instant expansion in his borrowing capacity followed. Small banks sprang into existence, and money (though not unfrequently at usurious interest) became freely obtainable by the most improvident peasantry in the world. Shop accounts were allowed to run, and small loads of debt were gradually accumulated by the farmers. The years of agricultural prosperity which followed 1870 led the farmer class to look hopefully on the future, and when the years of depression ensued they were dragged down not only by the failure of their source of income, but also by an ever increasing load of debt, which nothing but perpetual prosperity could have enabled them to discharge[3].

[1] Richmond Commission.
[2] See *ante*, page 137.

[3] And see on this subject Richey, pp. 98, 99.

On the 29th of July 1880 the second Commission[1] issued, appointing a special examination into the working of the Act of 1870. It is doubly important, both as showing the state of landed relations in Ireland as affected by this Act, and also as furnishing the basis of the Act of 1881 in which Mr Gladstone again dealt with the land question. Most of the reasons advanced by the Bessborough Commission to account for the failure of the former Act have been dealt with in the last chapter, the increase of rents, the insecurity of tenure still existing, the inadequacy of the compensation given, its unsuitability to meet the needs of the tenant, and other faults. The evidence with which these propositions are illustrated is both clear and voluminous, and shows in addition how critical the situation really was with which the Legislature was about to grapple.

The Commissioners again differed considerably in the view they took of the land question, but in their principal report[2] they stated that the method of the Act of 1870, by which the tenant's interest was dealt with by indirect means, was not suitable. They went on to point out that the distinction drawn between tenancies under Ulster custom and other tenancies was a mistake: and stated that the Ulster custom, as legalized, had failed, showing the same weak points as characterised the land law of the rest of Ireland. They suggested "that in future the same land law should prevail throughout Ireland, and that the yearly tenants, in every part of the kingdom, should possess the same rights and be subject to the same obligations[3]." Finally they advocated a change of the law based on the concession to the tenant of 'Fixity of Tenure,' 'Fair Rent' and 'Free Sale'—that is, the notorious three F's.

On the 7th of April Mr Gladstone, on a motion for leave to

---

[1] The Bessborough Commission.

[2] Five Commissioners were appointed, viz. The Earl of Bessborough, Baron Dowse, The O'Connor Don, Mr William Shaw and Mr Kavanagh. The main report was signed by all save Mr Kavanagh (who gave a separate report),

but the O'Connor Don and Mr Shaw also sent in supplementary reports expressing different views as to the remedy to be adopted for admitted evils.

[3] Report of Bessborough Commission, pp. 13—39.

bring in the Land Law (Ireland) Bill 1881, explained in a lengthy speech the lines on which it was proposed to legislate, amounting shortly to a recognition of the three F's and the creation of a special Court for the purposes of the Act. On the 22nd of August 1881 the Act, 44 & 45 Vict. c. 49, became law. Besides many blots in this celebrated Statute, which will be treated of in detail when considering its provisions, it may at the outset be stated that there is much reason to believe that a more advantageous step would have been taken had the previous Acts been completely repealed, and a new, rather than an amending, Statute passed. The paralyzing subtlety of the Act of 1881 was largely increased by its enactments being supplementary rather than final; while the process rendering the invocation of the action of the Court necessary was eminently unsuitable to the condition of the country. The prevailing influence of the combination of agitators which has been exerted against the Act; the ingrained distaste of the peasantry to trust themselves in the hands of the law; the widespread feeling that time will bring even larger concessions[1]; and the cost involved in making the application, have all contributed to prevent the tenants resorting largely to the Courts.

The length of the Act prevents the possibility of giving a full summary of its provisions, but its principal features are as follows. First, dealing with the subject of free sale, the tenant for the time being of every holding not specially excepted[2] was enabled to sell his tenancy for the best price he could get[3], pro-

---

[1] See 2nd article on the *Land System of Ireland*, by his Honour Judge O'Connor Morris. *Law Quarterly Review*, January, 1888.

[2] The definition of tenant given in sec. 57 excludes middlemen; and notice the tenancies which are excepted by sec. 58 from the operation of the Act (save as regards part v, and in so far as it amends the Act of 1870 with regard to improvements), viz. (1) any holding not agricultural or pastoral; (2) demesne lands and town parks; (3) any holding let for pasture and valued at not less than £50 per annum; (4) holdings let for pasturage when the tenant is non-resident; (5) holdings in virtue of being a hired labourer or servant; (6) lettings in conacre, etc.; (7) holdings let to tenant whilst retaining any office or employment, or for temporary convenience or necessity (provided there be contract in writing showing the object of the letting); (8) cottage allotments not exceeding half an acre; (9) glebes.

[3] 44 & 45 Vict. c. 49, sec. 1.

vided that certain regulations were complied with[1]. Of these the principal were that it should be sold, save with the consent of the landlord[2], to one person only; that the proposed new tenant was not refused by the landlord on reasonable grounds[3]; and that notice was given by the tenant to the landlord of his intention to sell[4], of the name of the purchaser, and of the consideration agreed on for the purchase[5]. The landlord on his part, on receiving notice of the intended sale, has the option of buying in the tenancy[6], and of refusing the new tenant on reasonable grounds[7], or if he fails to satisfy acknowledged claims against the outgoing tenant for arrears of rent, or for breaches of covenant[8]. When he receives notice of an intended sale the landlord, if he is not desirous of purchasing the tenancy "otherwise than as a means of securing the payment of any sums due to him for arrears of rent or other breaches of the contract or conditions of tenancy," if the tenant proceeds with the sale may purchase the tenancy for the sum he claims, provided no purchaser is found to give the same or more[9].

As regards the question of improvements, when any of a permanent nature have been made by the landlord they may, if he consents, be sold with the holding, and he will be entitled to the portion of the purchase-money obtained by their sale[10]. The

---

[1] And subject to the provisions of the Act as to the sale of a tenancy under statutory conditions.

[2] 44 & 45 Vict. c. 49, sec. 1, sub-sec. (1); and by sec. 2 the tenant from year to year was prohibited from subdividing or subletting his holding without the consent in writing of the landlord.

[3] Sec. 1, sub-sec. (6).

[4] Sec. 1, sub-sec. (2).

[5] Sec. 1, sub-sec. (4).

[6] Sec. 1, sub-sec. (3). The price to be agreed upon, or in event of disagreement to be settled by the Court. Where the landlord purchases a present holding neither by the wish of the tenant nor in open market, if the holding is re-let within 15 years from the passing of the Act to another tenant it is subject to the provisions regulating present tenancies. Sec. 20, sub-sec. (3). See post p. 162 (note 4).

[7] Sec. 1, sub-sec. (6).

[8] Sec. 1, sub-sec. (9). By sub-sec. (15) any sum payable to the landlord out of the purchase-money is a first charge thereon. By sub-sec. (7) in the case of a sale by a landlord on account of a breach of a statutory condition, the Court has power to grant payment of debt, arrears, or damages to the landlord from the purchase-money.

[9] 44 & 45 Vict. c. 49, sec. 1, sub-sec. (16).

[10] 44 & 45 Vict. c. 49, sec. 1, sub-sec. (8), and said improvements are then

tenant who has sold his tenancy on quitting his holding is not entitled to receive compensation for improvements or for disturbance[1]. Ulster tenant-right customs are not interfered with; the tenant can sell either under the usage or under the Act as he thinks best[2]; but if a tenancy subject to Ulster, or similar usage, be sold under the Act the tenancy remains subject to the custom unless it has been purchased by the landlord[3].

The Act then proceeds to a series of provisions by which the tenant is able to commute his tenure into a protected term for fifteen years, and which is in fact renewable without limit. The way in which this was achieved was in the highest degree ingenious, but the very elaboration of its details hindered practical efficiency. Dealing first with the case where an increase of rent is demanded by the landlord from the tenant of a present tenancy[4] (or in the case of a future tenancy where the landlord demands an increase of rent beyond the amount fixed at its commencement), it provides that if the tenant *agrees* to continue his holding at the higher rent his tenancy is for the term of fifteen years regulated by what are termed *statutory conditions*[5]. These are: that[6] provided the tenant

(1)   duly pays his rent,

(2)   does not commit persistent waste,

(3)   does not (without the consent in writing of the landlord) subdivide or sublet the holding, or erect any dwelling-house thereon, save as provided in the Act, otherwise than in substitution for those already there at the date of the passing of the Act,

deemed to have been made by the purchaser.

[1] Sec. 1, sub-sec. (11). And a tenant who has received compensation for disturbance or improvement is not entitled at the same time to sell his tenancy.

[2] Sec. 1, sub-sec. (12), and see *post* p. 163, 164 for new scale of compensation, etc.

[3] Sec. 1, sub-sec. (13).

[4] That is, one subsisting at the time of the passing of the Act, or created before the first of January, 1883, in a holding in which a tenancy was subsisting at the time of the Act passing. And every tenancy to which the Act applies is deemed a present tenancy until the contrary is proved. Sec. 57.

[5] Sec. 4, sub-sec. (1). The term of 15 years is called a *statutory term*.

[6] Sec. 5.

(4) does not, by any Act, cause the holding to vest in an assignee in bankruptcy,

(5) permits the entrance of the landlord to cut timber, mine, shoot, etc.,

(6) does not, without consent, open any house on the holding for the sale of intoxicating liquors,

he shall not be compelled to pay any higher rent than that settled at the commencement of his statutory term, and shall not be ousted from the holding, save for breach of one of the statutory conditions. The landlord also is prohibited from taking proceedings to compel the tenant to quit his holding for breach of any of the statutory conditions save as follows (a) where the condition broken is that of due payment of rent he can proceed by ejectment, (b) where the condition broken is any other statutory condition, then by ejectment founded on notice to quit[1], the Court being allowed to grant relief against forfeiture upon payment of damages or otherwise, if it should appear equitable[2].

If on the increase of rent being proposed the tenant *refuses* to pay the higher rate he may claim compensation for disturbance if he is compelled to abandon the holding by notice to quit and does not sell the tenancy[3]. The Act of 1881 provides an amended scale of compensation for disturbance[4], which is, as regards all tenancies above the annual rental of £10, higher than the scale given in the Act of 1870[5], and is also more equitable, as not only is the amount of compensation regulated with regard to the rent paid, but the classes of holdings are

---

[1] 44 & 45 Vict. c. 49, sec. 13, sub-sec. (3) b.

[2] See Field, p. 333, and 44 & 45 Vict. c. 49, sec. 13, sub-sec. (3) & (4). A tenant compelled to quit his holding during the continuance of a statutory term in his tenancy, in consequence of a breach by him of a statutory condition, lost his right to compensation for disturbance, sec. 13, sub-sec. (6): but by sec. 20, sub-sec. (4), if he held under the Ulster tenant-right custom he was entitled to the benefit of the custom despite the termination of his tenancy

by breach of a statutory condition. The purchaser of a present tenancy sold in consequence of a breach of a statutory condition was not entitled to claim a judicial rent, but might hold at a previously settled rent for the remainder of the statutory term. This applies also to the case of a tenancy not subject to statutory conditions in case of a similar breach. Sec. 20.

[3] Sec. 4 sub-sec. (3), and sec. 6.

[4] Sec. 6.

[5] The limit of £250 as the maximum of compensation was abolished.

also regulated in the same way. The faults pointed out therefore in the compensation clauses of the Act of 1870 (where in the case of two tenants holding farms of the same valuation, but one paying more rent than the other, the absurd result was reached that the tenant who paid less rent, and hence had the most valuable interest in his holding, was primâ facie entitled to the smaller compensation for losing his farm[1]) are avoided, and a more reasonable measure of compensation afforded. In addition, section 3 of the Act of 1870 was amended by the striking out of the words " for the loss which the Court shall find to be sustained by him by reason of quitting his holding," so that the tenant is entitled to such compensation as the Court, in view of all the circumstances of the case thinks proper, subject of course to the scale of compensation given in the Act of 1881.

A further protection is given to the tenant in that his right to sell his holding is not barred by the landlord having taken proceedings to compel him to quit; for at any time before six months from the execution of a writ or decree for possession in an ejectment for non-payment of rent[2] he may sell his tenancy, and if sold it is held to be an existing tenancy despite these proceedings[3].

As regards compensation for improvements also a step further is taken. The provisions of the Act of 1870 had rendered it possible for a landlord in many cases by changing the rent of a holding, or by a slight alteration of the holding, to create a new tenancy, even though the same tenant remained in possession, and hence to bar the claim of the tenant to compensation[4]; but the Act of 1881 prevents the creation of such a new tenancy from rendering void the right to compensation[5].

---

[1] See *ante*, pp. 146, 147.

[2] And he might also sell his tenancy at any time before, but not after, the execution of such writ or decree in any other ejectment than for non-payment of rent. Sec. 13 (1). And within the same periods, if the decree has been obtained before the Act, the tenant may apply to the Court to fix the judicial rent of the holding.

[3] The landlord's rights, if the tenancy is not redeemed within six months, being however preserved. Sec. 13, sub-sec. (1).

[4] This was rendered possible by the construction given to the words " made by himself (the tenant) or his predecessors in title." See Field, p. 317, 318, and 333, and *Irish Land Acts*, by G. McDermot.

[5] 44 & 45 Vict. c. 49, sec. 7.

If the tenant whose rent the landlord proposes to raise does not wish to accept the increase the Act provides also another remedy for him[1]. This remedy varies according as the tenancy is a present[2] or a future one[3]. (1) In the case of a *present* tenancy the tenant can make an application to the Court to fix the fair rent[4] for the holding. This right to get a fair rent fixed, moreover, is not confined to the case where the landlord desires to raise the rent of the holding; for by section 8[5], *the tenant of any present tenancy* to which the Act applies, or such tenant and the landlord jointly, or the landlord when he has failed to come to an agreement with the tenant, *may apply to the Court to fix the fair rent of the holding.* When the judicial rent has been fixed by the Court, then for fifteen years the tenancy becomes one subject to statutory conditions[6]. During that time the rent cannot be altered[7]: while even if proceedings have been taken to compel the tenant to quit his holding, and are pending before the application of the tenant to the Court to fix a judicial rent is disposed of, the Court has the power to postpone or suspend such proceedings till the question of the judicial rent is settled[8]. In the case of a present tenancy also, which is not a statutory term, the landlord and tenant, if they agree in writing as to what is then a fair rent for the holding and file the agreement in Court, can commute the tenancy into a statutory term[9]. (2) In the case of a *future* tenancy the tenant, if he refuses to pay an increase of rent demanded by the landlord, may sell the tenancy, which is then

---

[1] See Field, p. 331.

[2] See *ante*, p. 162, note (4).

[3] i.e. created after the passing of the Act.

[4] Sec. 8 (1). By sub-sec. 5, moreover, the Court may also on application fix the value of the holding, and then if during the term the tenant gives notice to sell, the landlord may purchase at that value plus any addition for extra improvements. This section does not apply to holdings under the Ulster custom.

[5] Sub-sec. (1).

[6] Sec. 8, sub-sec. (3).

[7] An application to the Court to determine a judicial rent may not be made except during the last twelve months of the current statutory term. Sec. 8, sub-sec. (8). But notice the interference with the 'fair rents' under the Act of 1887. It was rendered necessary by the severe agricultural depression. See *post* p. 180, 181.

[8] Sec. 13, sub-sec. (3).

[9] Sec. 8, sub-sec. (6). A similar agreement may be made during the last twelve months of a statutory term.

to be sold subject to the increased rent, and the tenant is entitled to receive from the landlord any sum by which the Court
shall decide the selling value of his tenancy to have been depreciated below what it would have fetched at a fair rent : while
in addition the Court may grant him the costs of the sale[1].

Under the Act of 1870 efforts were made to force the hand
of the landlord, and to make him in his own interest create
leases for a term of not less than 31 years[2]. The Act of 1881
also offered facilities for the creation of terms of this kind;
enacting that, if the tenant of a tenancy to which the Act
applies is not in possession of either a statutory or a fixed
tenancy, a lease by agreement between the landlord and such
tenant for not less than 31 years shall, when sanctioned by the
Court, become a 'judicial lease' and lie outside the provisions of
the statute[3].

Yet another species of tenure might be created under the
Act of 1881 by agreement between landlord and tenant, and
substituted for that previously existing in the holding, namely,
what is described as a 'fixed tenancy[4].' The conditions of this
kind of holding are mainly dependent on the agreement between the parties, subject to the proviso that the tenant (1)
pays a fee-farm rent[5], and (2) is not to be compelled to leave
his holding save on breach of a statutory condition.

The result of the provisions as to fixity of tenure[6] which

---

[1] 44 & 45 Vict. c. 49, sec. 4, sub-
sec. (2).

[2] See *ante*, pp. 137, 138.

[3] 44 & 45 Vict. c. 49, sec. 10.
These provisions apply also to the proposed tenant of any holding to which
the Act applies and which is not subject to a subsisting tenancy. See also
Field, p. 336 and 337. The question
naturally arises, what would be the
position of a present tenant, who
changed his yearly tenancy for such a
lease, upon its termination? In answer
to this sec. 10 of the Act provides that
" at the expiration of a judicial lease
made to the tenant of a present tenancy
and for a term not exceeding 60 years,

the lessee shall be deemed to be the
tenant of a present ordinary tenancy"
(i.e. one neither (a) subject to statutory
conditions, nor (b) to a judicial lease, nor
(c) a fixed tenancy, but which is within
the Act. See sec. 5) "from year to year
at the rent and subject to the conditions of the lease, so far as such conditions are applicable to such tenancy."

[4] Sec. 11.

[5] Sec. 12. This rent may or may
not be subject to revision once in 15
years as agreed between landlord and
tenant.

[6] Fixity of tenure was of course also
aided by the improved rules for compensation for disturbance.

have been dealt with, therefore, is in short that a tenant under
the Act can (1) on an increase of rent being proposed by the
landlord and accepted by the tenant, or (2) in the case of a
present tenancy without an increase having been proposed, by
application to the Court commute his tenancy into a statutory
term; while in the case of leases for more than 31 years, and
of fixed tenancies, the agreement of the landlord and tenant
without litigation becomes binding[1].

A large equitable power was vested in the Court by the
provision[2] which enacted that on the hearing of any application of a landlord or tenant, if the Court was of opinion that
the conduct of either party had been unreasonable, the application
might be (1) refused, or (2) granted subject to conditions; and
that the offending party might be penalized in costs. The
Court also had power, in the case of leases existing at the time
of the passing of the Act, where unjust terms had been imposed upon the tenant on his acceptance of the said lease after
the passing of the Act of 1870, to set aside the lease on the
application[3] of the tenant and place him on the same footing as
that occupied by the holder of an ordinary tenancy[4].

It will be remembered that under the Act of 1870 the
Board of Works was authorized to advance two-thirds of the
price of the holding to a tenant desirous of purchasing, and it
has been pointed out that (despite this being increased by

---

[1] See Field, p. 338. And it should
be noticed that by sec. 20, sub-sec. (2),
where the landlord resumes possession
of a present tenancy and reinstates the
tenant, such tenancy again becomes
subject to the provisions of the Act as
regards present tenancies, and if the
parties agree at the time of the re-
instatement as to rent to be paid it
becomes a judicial rent.

[2] Sec. 9.

[3] Such application to be made within
six months of the passing of the Act of
1881. See Field 339, and 44 & 45
Vict. c. 49, sec. 21.

[4] But the tenant of a holding of
more than £150 annual value was able
by a written agreement to contract
himself out of the operation of either
of the Acts. In another case also
a contract inconsistent with the Acts
is allowed, for by sec. 22, when a holding subject to customary rights has
been purchased by the landlord by
voluntary purchase before the Act of
1881, and the owner is in actual occupation; at the date of the passing of
the Act then in a first tenancy of
the holding subsequently created by
written agreement the tenancy may
be exempted from the provisions of
sec. 1 as to free sale. 44 & 45 Vict. c.
49, sec. 22.

the Act of 1872[1] to two-thirds of the *value* of the holding) these purchase clauses failed signally. The new purchase clauses of the Act of 1881 also provided for the advance of money to the purchasing tenant, but regulated the advances in a different way. The Land Commission was empowered[2], if satisfied with the security, to advance[3] sums to the purchasing tenant to the following amounts.

1. If the tenant is about to purchase from the landlord for a principal sum—then not more than three-fourths of such sum.

2. If the tenant purchases by paying a fine and engaging to pay a fee-farm rent—then any sum not exceeding one half of the fine, on condition that the fee-farm rent is not more than seventy-five per cent. of what the Commissioners think a fair rent for the holding.

And the Act further sought to facilitate sales to the tenants by allowing the Commission under certain conditions to purchase estates from the landlords and to sell them again to the tenants[4]; and by allowing the Commission to indemnify the tenant purchasers of an incumbered estate against incumbrances[5].

This then being an outline of the provisions[6] of the celebrated Act of 1881, which again remodelled the whole of the system of agricultural holdings in Ireland, it is possible in the light of after events to detect many flaws and also to observe many good points. The Act, as has been pointed out, was greatly marred for practical purposes by its own subtlety, and in addition the details as to procedure proved at first to work but indifferently, and complaints were made that the judgments as to improvements, etc. by the Commissioners were

---

[1] 35 & 36 Vict. c. 32, sec. 1, subsec. (1).

[2] 44 & 45 Vict. c. 49, sec. 24, subsec. (1).

[3] Such advances to be repaid by an annuity in favour of the Land Commission for 35 years of £5 for every hundred advanced, and so in proportion for every less sum, sec. 28; and

until the whole charge was paid off the tenant might not subdivide or let his holding without consent. Sec. 30, sub-sec. (1) a.

[4] Sec. 26, sub-sec. (1); and see Field, p. 341.

[5] Sec. 26, sub.-sec. (5).

[6] See *post* p. 179 note 1 as to provisions for emigration.

not sufficiently specific to set vexed questions finally at rest[1].

A large amount of criticism was focused on the Act, and various objections to its principle were raised. It was urged that (apart even from what many considered a most unwarrantable inroad on the rights of the landlord[2]) a dual ownership was established in the soil, a thing which was termed radically evil. Yet this dual ownership is to be found all over Europe, and Ulster tenant-right presents about the one satisfactory feature of the land history of Ireland. Again, another body of the opponents of the Act deplored the vanished rights of the landlord, which they declared to be now reduced to a rent-charge on his estates. Yet he still possessed the remedies of distress, ejectment, action, and injunction; while he had a right to enter on the tenant's land for the purpose of mining, quarrying, hunting[3], etc.; possessed rights to woods and minerals, held the reversion of the tenant's estate, and had a right every fifteen years to a revision of rent[4]. It was stated that the principle of the Act was adverse to the making of improvements by the landlord; but where most of the holdings are small, and the works are therefore usually the result of the labour of the tenant, this does not apply as it would in a country where large farms and valuable holdings are the rule[5].

Another class of objections was, that no Government[6] machinery could properly value rents, which were purely local matters and could only be settled fairly by persons intimately acquainted with the particular district under consideration; that the landlord would still incur odium by having to resort to eviction on breach of the statutory conditions; that the rent

---

[1] See Report of Select Committee of the House of Lords, 1882.

[2] And without expressing an opinion as to whether the exigencies of the Irish situation made the recognition of tenant-rights in the land imperative or not, there is no doubt that his rights were largely restricted.

[3] Sec. 5, sub-sec. (5).

[4] O'Connor Morris, *Land System of Ireland*, part II. *L. Q. Review*, January, 1888.

[5] Ibid.

[6] This objection was urged by Mr Bonamy Price in his special report on the Richmond Commission.

which would be fair from a poor tenant would be too small if paid by a richer one; and that despite the provisions against subdivision and subletting, the ultimate effect of the Act would be to increase or at least perpetuate 'starvation holdings.'

In all of these last objections there lies a germ of truth, but none of them were sufficiently developed to cause serious harm, and had the Act succeeded in other ways it would have compensated for the smaller evils caused. Unfortunately the purchase clauses, which were held the most vital portion of the measure, failed completely. The Select Committee of the House of Lords, which in 1882 examined the working of the Act, cast some light on the reason of this failure[1], the evidence tending to show that the Land Commission should be empowered to advance the whole purchase-money[2] of his holding to the tenant to render purchase possible; the amount which might be advanced under the Act being insufficient. The Committee themselves[3] ascribed the failure of the purchase clauses to the fact, that:—

1. When a limited owner sold to a tenant the money passed into Chancery, and was invested on the low interest of Government Stock, while the expenses of the process were heavy.

2. When the land is subject to a quit rent[4], all the holdings into which any estate is divided remain liable for it, the Commissioners not being able to apportion, &c.

3. "Under the present arrangements there is no sufficient inducement to the tenant to purchase his holding at any price at which the owner would be likely to sell it;" this arising not so much from the fault of the provisions for purchase as from the singularly good position of the tenant of a statutory term.

[1] It must be remembered that this Committee was appointed in the face of the opposition of the House of Commons, and represented practically the landlord interest. A preliminary report was published but not a final one, as the evidence of the sub-commissioners working under the Act could not be obtained, owing to their duties keeping them in Ireland.

[2] The Committee suggested that the loans should be advanced at 3 per cent. or 4 per cent.

[3] Preliminary Report of the Select Committee, 1882, Parliamentary Papers Vol. VIII.

[4] And nearly one-third of the land of Ireland was so subject.

It is undeniable that the efforts of the agitation, which has exerted such an influence on the minds and methods of the Irish peasantry, has been employed rather against the acceptance by the tenantry of the advantages of the Act, while it has pointedly prevented the working of the provisions for free sale[1]. As a result the Act of 1881 has failed to allay the popular discontent, and the tenantry have on the whole made scanty use of its provisions. A very large number of applications to fix fair rents[2] have indeed been made, but during the first year of the Act only forty cases of application for judicial leases[3] came before the Court, and during the same period only 85 tenants made use of the purchase clauses. In some ways this would tend to show that the question of fair rent is the one which tenants regard as being of the most vital importance, and would rather militate against the idea that they are eager to possess the fee of the soil.

The position of the agricultural tenants in Ireland under the Acts of 1870 and 1881 is certainly remarkable; for their tenure, which before these Acts was marked by complete uncertainty, has been changed to one in the highest degree favourable to the tenant. The attempt to reconcile law and fact by constructing statutes on the basis of the ideas and expectations of the tenantry has been carried to a remarkable extent, and the position of the Irish tenant from year to year is absolutely unique in the manner in which it is fenced and protected by legislation, until it greatly resembles a tenancy in perpetuity. Despite the faults which have been pointed out in the Acts of over-subtlety and want of finality, it is hard not to believe that they contain within them the groundwork of a satisfactory settlement of the land question.

[1] See O'Connor Morris, *L. Q. Review*, 1888.

[2] See Field, p. 357. No less than 80,187 notices to fix being lodged in the first year of the Act.

[3] "Three leases only were executed and sealed during the year. Twenty applications for fixed tenancies, two of which were withdrawn, while 15 were pending and three had been granted, and the necessary documents sealed." See Field, p. 357, from Report of the Irish Land Commissioners of the first year's working of the Act.

CHAPTER XII.

RECENT LEGISLATION.

No sooner had the Act of 1881 granted to the Irish tenant a degree of legislative protection unexampled in the history of English law than popular demands again became heard, and it was apparent that instead of solving the agrarian difficulty the Act had but whetted the desire for further concession. Two objects were now aimed at by even the more moderate of the tenants, (1) the abolition of arrears, and (2) the creation of an absolute peasant proprietary. The political complications of 1882 are too much concerned with present controversial politics to fall within the scope of this essay. But, whatever the cause, the state of Ireland was most critical. The 'no rent' agitation which has met with such universal condemnation had been started at the end of 1881; and the following year was marked by a ghastly catalogue of crime, while disorder and disaffection ran riot through the land.

On the 15th of May 1882 Mr Gladstone introduced to Parliament a Bill dealing with arrears. It had been the complaint of the tenants in Ireland that despite the provisions of the Act of 1881 their liability to eviction had not been lessened owing to the burden of arrears of rent which incumbered them, and they stated that large numbers of evictions on this ground were taking place. On the second reading of the Arrears Bill, Mr Gladstone admitted that the interference of the Legislature with respect to arrears of rent was exceptional and extraordinary[1], and that neither on economic nor constitutional principles could State interference by compulsion and gifts with

---

[1] Hansard, 3rd series, CCLXIX. p. 1270.

the settlement of debts be advocated[1]; but he urged in favour of the measure that it might prevent the failure[2] of one portion of the Land Act, and on the 18th of August the Arrears Act[3] received the Royal Assent.

This Act was confined in its operation to the tenants of holdings falling within the Act of 1881 and under the value of £30 per annum[4]. Its most important provision was, that if it could be proved to the satisfaction of the Land Commission (1) that the tenant of such a holding on or before the 30th of November 1882 had paid his rent for the year ending in 1881, (2) that antecedent arrears of rent were due by him to the land-lord, and (3) that he could not discharge them without losing his holding or being deprived of the means of duly cultivating it[5], an order for payment might be made by the Land Commission to or for the benefit of the landlord of one half of the arrears due (provided that the sum so paid did not exceed the yearly rent to which the holding was liable in the year preceding that ending in 1881). When the order for the payment of such a sum had been made the antecedent arrears were swept away, as also any judgment, decree or security for the rent; whilst any judgment or decree for the recovery of the holding on the ground of non-payment of rent was vacated as far as regarded any rent due in respect of the holding before the last gale day of the year ending in 1881, but not as regarded rent which had since that date accrued due[6]. The difference between this Act and the arrears clause of the Act of 1881[7] is very marked.

---

[1] See *Annual Register*, 1882, p. 80.

[2] Hansard, 3rd series, CCLXIX. p. 1274, "Without the settlement of this question I sorrowfully confess that the working of the Land Act, however beneficial, must remain essentially in-complete."

[3] 45 & 46 Vict. c. 47.

[4] The number of tenancies in Ireland which would fall under the limit of the £30 valuation was calculated at 585,000.

[5] 45 & 46 Vict. 47, sec. 1. The sale-able value of the tenant's interest be-

ing as far as appeared reasonable to the Commissioners taken into account in considering the tenant's power of paying, sec. 1, sub-sec. (2).

[6] Sec. 1, sub-sec. (2); but if the tenancy is sold within seven years the arrears dealt with and not satisfied shall, to an amount not exceeding one year of such arrears nor half the pro-fits of such a sale, be a sum payable to the landlord within the meaning of the Act of 1881.

[7] 44 & 45 Vict. c. 49, sec. 59. When advances had already been made under

The money provided by the Government (and which was supplied from the Irish Church Surplus) was given not as a loan but as a free gift, enforceable by either landlord or tenant. Applications for relief under the Act[1] were to be made before the end of 1882[2].

Even when aided by the Arrears Act the Act of 1881 did not work satisfactorily; the applications under its purchase clauses were few; and discontent was widely prevalent throughout the Irish agricultural peasantry. The skilful manipulation of political agitators both fostered the existing dissatisfaction and rendered nugatory the working of the Acts. The agricultural returns showed increasing depression, and the panacea of a tenant proprietary was widely urged. In 1884 two measures of land purchase were proposed by Mr Barry and Mr Dickson, and though they were rejected a promise was extorted from the Government to introduce a land purchase Bill. This pledge was redeemed by the introduction of Sir George Trevelyan's[3] scheme of land purchase, proposing an advance of £20,000,000 from the Imperial Exchequer, of which not more than 5,000,000 was to be advanced in any one year. The Bill was based on the idea of twenty years' purchase, and provided (1) that if the tenant would pay a quarter of the purchase-money the other three-quarters should be advanced by the State at such low interest that by the payment of an annual sum, not exceeding his present rent, for forty years he would become the freeholder; while (2) if no principal sum were paid by him the whole of the purchase-money might be advanced

this section the Commissioners were empowered by sec. 15 of the Act of 1882 to abolish the rent-charge on proof that tenant was at the time when the advance was made unable to discharge the arrears.

[1] Sec. 10, but in certain cases time might be extended to April 30, 1883.

[2] Another Act of this year, the Labourers' Cottages and Allotments (Ireland) Act, 1882, 45 & 46 Vict. c. 60, enabled the Land Commissioners, where the landlord and tenant had filed an agreement as to the fair rent of a holding is filed to make an order as to the accommodation of the labourers employed on the holding (sec. 3).

[3] Then Mr Trevelyan. When he brought forward the Bill he stated, " That land in Ireland was almost unsaleable, the 'block' being as great as it was when Sir Robert Peel passed the Incumbered Estates Act." *Annual Register*, 1884, p. 190—192.

at 5 per cent. to be paid for thirty-three years, but in this case he was obliged to satisfy the local board as to security, and a guarantee was expected out of the local cess.

This Bill, the provisions of which as will be observed were of a most sweeping character, was eventually dropped; but in the following year Lord Ashbourne, the Lord Chancellor for Ireland, introduced the Purchase of Land (Ireland) Act 1885[1]. It amended the purchase clauses of the Act of 1881[2] by allowing an advance to the tenant of the whole purchase-money of his holding at 4 per cent.[3], to run for 49 years; and the protection of a cash guarantee was obtained by the State by the Commissioners retaining one-fifth of the money till the borrower repaid of the whole loan a sum equal to such fifth. The sum to be advanced by the State was limited to £5,000,000, and the working of the Act was placed in the hands of the Irish Land Commission[4].

Four large schemes of land purchase have therefore now been applied to Irish land with the object of enabling occupying tenants to become owners. The proposals of Mr Gladstone for drastic purchase in 1886 are both too much concerned with controversial politics and too unreal in their nature to come within the scope of this essay; but as it is evident how important a feature of the land law of Ireland is concerned in the working of those purchase clauses which have actually resulted in the creation of peasant freeholders, the comparison of the working of the Irish Church Act[5], the Bright clauses of the Act of 1870[6], tho purchase clauses of the Act of 1881[7] and Lord Ashbourne's Act[8] is highly instructive.

The following table is based on the statement made in the House of Commons on the 19th of November, 1888, by the Solicitor-General for Ireland[9]:

[1] 48 & 49 Vict. c. 73.

[2] 44 & 45 Vict. c. 49.

[3] Instead of three-quarters at 5 per cent.

[4] Power being given to appoint two new Commissioners, sec. 17.

[5] 32 & 33 Vict. c. 42, amended by 44 & 45 Vict. c. 71.

[6] 33 & 34 Vict. c. 46.

[7] 44 & 45 Vict. c. 49.

[8] 48 & 49 Vict. c. 73.

[9] Mr Madden, see Hansard, 3rd series, Vol. 330, pp. 1520—1531.

Act.	No. of Purchasers.	Amount advanced.
Irish Church Act	6,000	£1,674,000[1]
Land Act, 1870	824	518,716
Land Act, 1881	731	240,554
Lord Ashbourne's Act[2] (1885)	8,632	5,986,000[3].

It will be observed that Lord Ashbourne's Act has been by far the most effectual. Its success indeed was considerably greater than is shown by the above figures, since the hands of the Commissioners were tied by the limitation of the funds at their disposal, and 5,706 transactions under its provisions were still pending. The total number of agreements for purchase signed being 14,338.

Two more tables, based on the same authority, will show respectively the nature of the farms already bought under this Act, and the distribution of the peasant proprietors established throughout Ireland under its provisions.

1. Nature of Farms created.		2. Distribution of Applications.	
Rental.	No. of Holdings purchased.		
Under £10	3,599	Ulster . . .	7,711
Between £10 and £30	3,234	Munster . .	2,730
„ £30 and £50	884	Leinster . .	2,336
Over £50	915	Connaught . .	1,561

From these figures it is evident that Lord Ashbourne's Act has been largely successful in inducing the tenants to purchase their holdings: and its further extension by another grant of £5,000,000, which seems certain to pass the present session of Parliament, will doubtless greatly facilitate the process[4].

[1] The figures in this case represent the gross amount of the purchase-money; the amount advanced would be about three-quarters of the gross amount.

[2] Figures brought up to Oct. 31, 1888.

[3] This sum does not represent the money which had then been actually advanced—Lord Ashbourne's Act only empowered the grant of £5,000,000—but the sum actually advanced plus the sum which would be necessary to meet the pending transactions, 5,706 in number.

[4] Since the above was written this grant has been passed by 51 & 52 Vict. c. 49.

The principle of a peasant proprietary seems now to be generally held to be the best solution of the Irish land question, and the gradual buying out of the interest of the landlords to be considered likely to benefit that country. For many years this has been the dream of not a few of those interested in Ireland, and the theory of compulsory purchase was favoured by Mill[1]; but while expressing the opinion with much reserve, owing to the weighty authorities in favour of the scheme, the author of this essay is very doubtful of the ultimate advantages of the system. That in the immediate present it works well is true, and the tenants certainly seem to become more prosperous and more peaceable when settled upon holdings of which they are themselves the proprietors. The banishment of capital, however, entailed by a widespread application of the scheme, and the improvident habits of the Irish peasantry (so different from those of the French small holders who are always appealed to as a triumphant example) offer fatal objections to the ultimate success of a universal plan of this kind in Ireland.

The following extract from Mr Kavanagh's special report on the Bessborough Commission shows most forcibly the evil possibilities of such a plan:

"Examples of the old perpetuity leases have been given us in evidence, where the lessees holding on grants for ever at a nominal rent, have been, so far as the question is practically concerned, in the same position as owners in fee; and the condition of those properties now has been cited as exemplifying what the result of peasant proprietors would be, and if they can be taken as a fair example of what the result of a future experiment in that direction would result in, I think that even the most ardent advocate of that scheme would not consider it as encouraging. By the evidence it is shown that very few of the representatives of the original lessees are now in possession; ruined by idleness and extravagance, their grants soon passed into the hands of mortgagees, who, looking only to gain, let and sublet, divided and subdivided their lands, till over-popu-

---

[1] See *England and Ireland*, J. S. Mill, and *Mr Mill's plan for the paci-* *fication of Ireland examined*, by Lord Dufferin, 1868.

lation with its consequent ills of never-ceasing want and periodical famine were stereotyped in those districts, and even in the few instances which remain of the representatives of the original lessees still continuing in possession, the condition is no better. It is shown that as occasion arose for each owner to make provision for his family, the same course was adopted, till the successive increase of each generation reduced the holdings to a size utterly inadequate to the support of those depending on them for even a bare subsistence[1]."

The author inclines to the opinion that a *sweeping* measure of land purchase would be, at any rate in its ultimate result, an evil; and is of opinion that the true solution of the difficulty lies rather in statutory terms such as those created under the Act of 1881. They constitute a severe inroad on the rights of the landlord, but they do not forcibly banish him from the land, nor do they compel him (as a compulsory land purchase system would do) either to retain his house and grounds while shorn of his estate, or to sell his demesne at something not much above prairie value. Moreover, they constitute a real approximation of law and fact, the statutory term resembling very much the nature of the tenants' assumed rights in the soil.

If the country were freed from the bondage of the gigantic organization of disaffection; if the Irish Land Acts of 1870, 1881 and 1887 were cleared of their technicalities and re-enacted in the form of one shorter and simpler Act; and if the modes of procedure were simplified and cheapened, the author believes that the question of agricultural tenures would be on the high-road to settlement. While if public money were freely granted in aid of drainage and other improvements of the land[2], and (though with caution) in the creation of a *limited*, solvent and industrious class of peasant proprietors, and in aid of improved provisions for emigration (free from the faults which characterized these provisions in the Act of 1881, and which the provisions inserted in the Arrears Act

[1] Report of Bessborough Commission, p. 62.
[2] The light railway and drainage Bills now before Parliament are examples of this kind of legislation, and should be widely beneficial.

did not satisfactorily mend[1]), the system would be greatly facilitated. It is impossible to say that the Act of 1881 has been tried under fair conditions, and the Act of 1887 is yet new.

This latter Act[2] was introduced to the House of Lords by the Earl of Cadogan[3], who touched on the report presented by the Commission on the Act of 1881[4], and stated that the Government was averse to again disturb more than was necessary the law of Irish land tenure. The provisions of the Act extended to leaseholders the advantages from which they were excluded under the Act of 1881. All such leaseholders—some 150,000—were enabled, if they desired, to apply to the Court and to ask for a judicial revision of rent; that is, they were placed in the same position as the tenants of 'present tenancies' under the Act of 1881[5]. A difference was also made in the position of middlemen, who were enabled, if the Court reduced the rents paid by their tenants, under certain circumstances to give up their leases[6]. By the Act of 1881[7] a middleman who was not in occupation, and hence could not claim the protection of the Act, was frequently, while liable for his own rent, injured by his tenants having fair rents fixed as against him. This state of affairs was also prejudicial to the sub-tenants, since if the middleman made default and the head landlord proceeded by ejectment, the tenants were only able to save themselves from eviction by paying the head rent in full, and though they could then proceed against the middleman, this was not a privilege of much value[8].

In order to stop the evictions[9] which had become so pain-

---

[1] The Act of 1881 (sec. 32) enabled the Land Commission to enter into agreements with persons representing a State, Colony or public body, but the applications which were received did not fulfil these conditions. The Arrears Act 1882 empowered Boards of Guardians to raise money for helping emigration, and sanctioned grants to them for this purpose. See Field, pp. 353, 354.

[2] 50 & 51 Vict. c. 33.

[3] March 31st, 1887, see Hansard, 3rd series, Vol. 313, pp. 1—27.

[4] Lord Cowper's Commission, appointed 29th Sept. 1886.

[5] 50 & 51 Vict. c. 33, sec. 1.

[6] 50 & 51 Vict. c. 33, sec. 8.

[7] 44 & 45 Vict. c. 49, sec. 57.

[8] *Key to the Land Act*, 1887, T. M. Healy, pp. 57, 60.

[9] Whether the provisions introduced were likely to have this effect is rather doubtful, but that this was the belief

fully prevalent, the Act of 1887 contained a provision which will be better understood if the state of the then law of ejectment is briefly considered. The tenant under a lease, or holding a yearly tenancy, was liable to eviction when one year's rent was in arrear. The fact that a judgment or decree in ejectment had been obtained did not however get rid of the tenant's claim to his holding until such judgment or decree was actually executed; until then, and also for six months after such execution, the tenant was able to redeem his holding if he paid the landlord's costs and the rent due[1]. It was therefore necessary, in order that the six months during which the tenant had an equity of redemption might begin to run, for the landlord to proceed to actual eviction, even if the tenant was afterwards to be re-admitted as a care-taker. The provisions of the Act of 1887[2] made it sufficient for the landlord to serve notice of the judgment, and *ipso facto*, on receipt of the notice, the tenant became a mere care-taker without having been evicted, and the six months' period of redemption began to run. Certain equitable provisions were also inserted, enabling the County Court to give time to the tenants to help them to meet their liabilities.

The Act of 1887 is but an extension of the Act of 1881, and there appears no doubt that the admission of leaseholders to the benefit of its provisions is a step in the right direction. Certain temporary changes in the judicial rents were also provided for. One of the recommendations of Earl Cowper's commission had been that a shorter period than fifteen years should be fixed for the revision of the judicial rents. There were many obvious disadvantages in so soon unhinging again the settlements of judicial rents which had been effected under the Act of 1881, at the same time the unforeseen and calamitous agricultural depression of 1885 and the following years, which caused even the judicial rents to be

and intention of the Government was stated by the Earl of Cadogan, who when introducing the Bill said, "I do not think I am overstating the case when I say that the effect of the pro-posed provision will be to reduce the number of evictions by one-half." Hansard, 3rd series, Vol. 313, p. 13.

[1] 23 & 24 Vict. c. 154, secs. 52—71.
[2] 50 & 51 Vict. c. 33, sec. 7.

impossible to the tenants, rendered some action imperative. The Act of 1887 dealt with the difficulty by providing for a temporary re-adjustment of the judicial rents. The Land Commission was directed to determine the necessary change for the current year, and to take similar steps in 1888 and 1889[1]. It seems probable that if an amount of social order can be introduced into Ireland sufficient to give the Act a fair trial, that it should ultimately be successful.

All remedial measures which are only adopted in a crisis of social disunion are likely to be at first only slightly successful; but it is probable that if a quieter future is in store for Ireland, the tenants will realise that they possess a security in their holdings which is quite unexampled, and that the troubled sea of Irish passions should gradually calm. Works of improvement, the increased development of the soil, and the help of State-aided emigration may all have to be called into play before the quiet level is reached, but it would seem that the basis of tenure has been satisfactorily dealt with.

Surely it is no baseless hope that on the horizon is seen the dawning flush of a day of peace for Ireland; that the future holds years of happiness and prosperity when that lovely land, shaking off like a dark cloud the past of misery, bloodshed and despair, may take that place in the roll of countries which the talent, the genius, the wit and the learning of her sons so well entitle her to.

---

[1] 50 & 51 Vict. c. 33, sec. 30. The power of varying the judicial rent was only given for these three years, at the end of which time the tenants will be liable to the original judicial rent for the remainder of the statutory term.

LIST OF STATUTES CITED.

PATENT AND CLOSE ROLLS, ETC.

INDEX.

Joint family of India, 3
Judicial rents, 165, 180, 181

Kernetty, 37
Kilkenny, Statute of, 52
Kinship, as basis of early community, 3, 6

de Lacy, Hugh, obtains grant of Meath, 44
Land, arable, 24, 34, 35; bonds, 79; free trade in, 124; League, 157; measures, Irish, 70 (note); pasture, 24, 33, 34; relation of mere Irish to the, after Cromwell's conquest, 89; system, earliest form of, 3, 4
Land Act 1870, 134—155; objects of, 136; faults of, 138, 139, 145, 147, 153—155
Land Act 1881, 156—171; law of improvements under, 161, 164; statutory terms, 162, 163; compensation for disturbance, 163; regulations as to fair rent, 165; fixed tenancies, 166; equitable power of Court, 167; advances under, 167, 168; purchase clauses of, 168, 170
Land Act 1887, 178, 179
Landed Estates Act, 112, 134
Landholding classes in early times, 15—18
Landlord and Tenant Law Amendment Act (Ireland) 1860, 124—134
Leases, became unpopular with landlords, 100, 101, 105; refused to settlers, 87; refused to Catholics, 86; judicial, 166, 171
Levellers, 34, 95
Licenses, 43 (note), 53 (note)
Limerick, Treaty of, 83
Livery, 27, 29
Livery of seisin, 87
London Companies as landowners, 126 (note)

Mac Bryan, Murrough, 69
Mac Murrough, Dermot, 42
Manaich tenants, 32

Manorial system, how tried in Ireland, 91, 92
Manufactures, Irish, repression of, 84, 85, 90, 93; increase of, 98
Meath, ancient appanage of Irish Royalty, 42; granted to Hugh de Lacy, 44
Mensal lands, 10, 30, 31
Merchant Navigation Act 1663, 85
Middlemen, 82, 93, 96, 98, 124, 148, 179
Mortuath, 18
Mosyorowne, 37
Mountjoy, 63
Munster, desolation of, after Desmond war, 60; enclosure of commons in, 94; plantation of, 60, 61

'No rent' agitation, 172
Notices to quit, 127, 132, 163

Oak boys, 96
O'Callaghan, Cahir, 69
O'Connell, 107, 118
O'Connor, Roderick, King of Connaught, 42; makes Treaty of Windsor with Henry II., 46
O'Donnell, revolt of, 62, 63
O'Neil, Hugh, Earl of Tyrone, revolt of, 62; forfeiture of estates of, 63, 73
Orkney, Lady, 84 (note)
Ormonde, Earl of, 92
Ownership, changes in nature of, 7
Oxford, Council at, 47

Palatine counties, grants of, 45, 92
Pandarus, 59 (note)
Papists, disabilities heaped on, 86
Parliament, Grattan's, 98; Papists prevented from sitting in, 85
Peel, Sir Robert, 118
Penal Code, 86, 87, 90, 95
Pembroke, Richard de Clare, Earl of, see Strongbow
Petition, to Edward I. from Colonists of the Pale, 50; to Henry V. from Colonists of the Pale, 54
Petty, Sir William, 79, 80, 89, 90